A.A.- How Alcoholics Anonymous

MW01067798

A.A.- How Alcoholics Anonymous Steals Your Soul

Indoctrinating America in 12 Easy Steps

Robert H. Warner

A.A.- How Alcoholics Anonymous Steals Your Soul

Copyright © 2012 **Robert H. Warner**

All rights reserved.

ISBN-10:1489599266
ISBN-13:9781489599261

DEDICATION

This book is dedicated to all of the people who tried to force me to worship their God. Without you, I wouldn't have realized that the more religious someone is, the more ruthless they are.

A.A.- How Alcoholics Anonymous Steals Your Soul

Robert H Warner

CONTENTS

A.A.- How Alcoholics Anonymous Steals Your Soul

CHAPTER 1
Alcoholics Anonymous IS A Religion

Alcoholics Anonymous is a religious organization that tricks its members into becoming religious zealots who dedicate their lives to faith-healing, rooting out sin and being Born Again. This book details that indoctrination using AAs own words.

My name is Robert Warner, and some years back I was ordered to attend Alcoholics Anonymous (AA). I was told by *everyone* that AA was a non-religious program to cure alcoholism and that alcoholism is a medically recognized 'disease', just the same as cancer or diabetes. This episode taught me a valuable lesson; that just because *everyone* tells you something, that doesn't make it true. Sometimes they lie.

I successfully sued the Orange County (New York) Department Of Probation to have mandatory attendance at Alcoholics Anonymous ruled an unconstitutional violation of the First Amendment to the United States Constitution, eventually proving that AA is an intensely religious program. I eventually won and mandatory AA was ruled illegal because of its religious nature but, because the US Supreme Court refused to hear the defendants appeal, the jurisdiction of the decision was limited to that of the Second Circuit of the United States Court of Appeals. As a result, I continue to read of people in our country being forced to attend Alcoholics Anonymous, a deeply religious faith-healing sect of Christianity. AA has been able to position itself as this state-mandated religion by promoting itself with a cynical, dishonest semantic deception; they classify themselves as *"spiritual, not religious"*. The point of this book is to deconstruct the Alcoholics Anonymous program to show how AA camouflages their religion as medicine, and the semantic trickery it employs to that end. The deconstruction is necessary because Alcoholics Anonymous is incredibly bold when they lie; when AA tells you to pray to God, and seek knowledge of His will and the strength to carry it out, they say that that isn't religious and that God can mean anything that you want it to mean (God "as we understand Him"). A careful deconstruction will counter that nonsense when it shows that the goal of the AA program is for you to love God and *"call Him by name"* once you become *"better able to understand Him"*.

I am writing this book because Alcoholics Anonymous plays people for fools, and I want to provide the best possible weapon to protect people from AA's fraud; knowledge. While many religions go to great lengths to convert people to their religion, even resorting to violence, murder, terrorism and war, AA is the only religion that actually hides their religious nature to lure people into their rituals while they convert them. This tactic has enabled them to insidiously weave themselves into the social, political and legal workings of our nation. By hiding the program's religious nature they have positioned themselves to have people ordered into their religion by the courts and psychiatric profession, with those people being under threat to their freedom and fortune. I was one of those forced into their churches and I successfully sued in Federal Court, eventually winning a judgment that declared no one can be forced to attend AA. The outrageous part of that battle, and the heart of the incredible dishonesty of Alcoholics Anonymous, is that I had to argue for a decade that praying to God is religious. The losing defendants adopted AA's obscene lie that praying to God is not religious. AA tells this to the member in order to buy them time to convert the prospect.

AA employs a graduated indoctrination. Having successfully convinced our courts as well as the medical and psychiatric profession to accept their religion as a treatment for alcoholism, they are able to get masses of people to attend their services either voluntarily or by force. This provides AA churches with a pre-packaged, captive audience that has no choice but to join in AA rituals. They are often given the choice of either joining the religion of Alcoholics Anonymous or being confined to a locked facility indefinitely. This is not rehabilitation; it is forced religious re-education.

Once a person is in the door for their first AA meeting, the membership prospect embarks upon a journey characterized by lies, deceit and fraud. A cornerstone of the fraud of Alcoholics Anonymous is perhaps the most cynical literary manipulation of modern times; "AA isn't religious, it's spiritual". The confusion caused by such a statement, which attains credence in the targeted person's mind because of the endorsement by the State, and medical professionals, is something that AA relies on. They explicitly direct their members to hide the religious nature of Alcoholics Anonymous in order to keep the prospect coming back, giving them detailed instructions on how to do so. We have lent the power, prestige and force of our nation's institutions to Alcoholics Anonymous to perpetrate this fraud. If a person is compelled to go, by either the courts or a treatment professional in the substance abuse industry, the force and impact of the lies and trickery are compounded by the legitimacy of these institutions. In order to gain that endorsement AA had to sidestep the separation of church and state, as well as patient right policies protecting freedom of religion. They achieve this by calling themselves "spiritual, not religious"; that, however, is a semantic word game and a fraud.

Not only is AA a religious organization, they have a very distinct religious doctrine; faith-healing. They want to indoctrinate unwitting (and often unwilling) people into their religion, so they jump through incredible linguistic hoops to hide their faith-healing doctrine from prospective members. That's the impetus to Alcoholics Anonymous calling its God a "Higher Power; to convince targets that AA is not religious while simultaneously converting them to faith-healing.

One main tactic that AA employs is to tell prospects that anything can be their Higher Power- a chair, a table or the group itself. They dedicate many pages to this obfuscation but at the end of the program they reveal what they truly mean by "Higher Power"; that you will learn to "love God and call Him by name". While they tell new prospects that no religious belief is required, in truth theirs is a deeply religious program that believes only in faith-healing. They declare that no human power can relieve alcoholism and that God could and would if He were sought. AA claims non-religiosity; in reality, Alcoholics Anonymous is a fundamentalist, faith-healing religion.

Alcoholics Anonymous is an organization of religious zealots who believe that their religion is the only truth and that if it doesn't cure you, that's your fault- the program never fails. If you have a "relapse" it's because you didn't work the Steps properly. This "can't fail" arrogance is ensconced in an incantation that is chanted at most meetings; "It works if you work it!" To Alcoholics Anonymous, their program is completely fail-proof and anytime that their program doesn't work it is because the person that it failed is "constitutionally incapable of being honest with themselves".

AA believes itself perfect because they have a direct line to God. They don't just teach that theirs is a good religion, but that God does their bidding; God can and will relieve your alcoholism if you follow AA religious teachings. AA is the only religion I know of that believes that it knows the mind of God, and that God will obey them. There is no concept of "if it is His will" in AA; for AA, God will do as He is told. If AA just kept their services voluntary, as every other religion in America does, this arrogant 'God-does-as-we-tell-Him-to' mentality would not be a problem. That, though, is not the case.

Alcoholics Anonymous has proven itself a danger to religious freedom. By billing themselves as non-religious treatment for what has been classified as a disease, even while they teach faith-healing, they have created a situation where people are compelled- be clear, I mean ordered and forced- to submit to this religious indoctrination. Having passed their faith-healing off to both the courts and the substance abuse treatment industry as medical treatment, a situation has been created where prospective members aren't allowed to believe what their own ears, intellect and common sense are telling them.

When one hears instructions to pray to God, and to ask for the knowledge of His will (always capitalized and always male) and the strength to carry it out, the immediate and clear understanding is that they have fallen into a religious study group. However, EVERYONE that the prospect talks to- their addiction treatment staff, courts, doctors, probation or parole officers- are telling them they are wrong; AA is the only treatment for their disease, and it is NOT religious. So the prospect keeps trying to understand the un-understandable; how can one pray to God without practicing religion? THAT is AA's meat and potatoes. AA counts on that confusion to give them time to convert people to their religion, to build their attendance rolls, to fill their pews. If the indoctrination doesn't take, well, that's OK; as long as they get their opportunity to convert a non-believer, who cares if the targets are there of their own free will?

The goal of Alcoholics Anonymous is religious indoctrination. They must convince you that all is lost without their God, their religion and their beliefs but they hide that goal because if someone who comes seeking what they were told was treatment for a disease finds a religious service instead, that person might walk away and never come back. Even if the prospect is a very religious person they might not take kindly to Alcoholics Anonymous trying to convert them from their own religion into the AA religion under the guise of medicine. AA's problem is truth, and that is what they must work around.

They do this by trying to convince prospective converts that AA's words have their own special meaning; that prayer isn't religious, that God isn't a supernatural being and that AA's religion isn't religious- its medicine. Working hand in hand with alcohol counselors, many of whom are AA members, this fraud is perpetrated until such a time that the prospect has, to some degree, been converted to AA's religion. As the conversion takes a stronger hold more of the truth is revealed until such a time that the conversion is complete and all of the subterfuge is dropped. Then, you find out AA's true philosophy as laid out in Step Twelve of the Twelve Steps and Twelve Traditions book (the 12x12); at the start they tell you that your "Higher Power" can be anything you want, even a chair, but by Step Twelve you will "learn to love God and call Him by name". If each new prospect reads all of the Alcoholics Anonymous books and literature before entering AA this fraud might not work (though it would have to be a very careful reading so as to see

11

past the misleading nature of AA's Step instructions); all of AA's religious concepts are contained within these publications (indeed, in this book I will base all of my assertions on AA's own published writings).

But that's not how AA works- you don't read AA, you do AA. Most people's introduction to Alcoholics Anonymous is achieved by attending a meeting, either voluntarily or by coercive force such as the courts, parole or probation and that is where the graduated indoctrination begins; all members of Alcoholics Anonymous are instructed to hide AA's religious nature from prospective members- to lie.

Members are taught that any non-believer in God is a belligerent savage who must be protected from what AA calls "prejudice" against belief in God. They are instructed to, at all cost, hide the fact that AA doctrine holds that the cure for alcoholism is God personally lifting the obsession to drink, that practicing AA doctrine triggers a miracle and that Alcoholics Anonymous has deduced the will, mind and intentions of God.

While on its face AA may seem quite compatible with most religion's tenets, I would suggest that it conflicts with many. If AA would simply put out an honest representation of its doctrine, people could make an intelligent and informed decision on whether or not to join this church. That is why I wrote this book; I hope that it will be a useful tool in counteracting the chicanery of Alcoholics Anonymous. To that end, I have written this book in six main sections; this introductory Chapter 1 and five more.

Chapter 2, 'The Twelve Step Indoctrination', is a detailed description, and dissection, of the graduated indoctrination process that AA employs.

Chapter 3, 'The Real Alcoholics Anonymous', is a synopsis of how Alcoholics Anonymous actually works.

Chapter 4, 'A Self Defense Primer', provides the reader with the true aim of the various AA lies they will be told in the course of AA's Twelve Steps with a means to rebut those lies; a counterpoint to a con if you will.

Chapter 5, 'The Danger of AA', is something that I hope will show how AA threatens the freedom of every American who does something that an employer or government official finds distasteful

Chapter 6, 'My Story Of A Self-Cured Alcoholic' is my view of how I rid myself of my problem and how I believe that my 'cure' can work for anyone.

I hope you will find this book useful and I wish you all of the best in your search for personal growth.

CHAPTER 2
The Twelve Step Indoctrination
----

1. We admitted we were powerless over alcohol that our lives had become unmanageable.

2. Came to believe that A Power Greater than Ourselves could restore us to sanity.

3. Made a decision to turn our will and our lives over to the care of God as we understood Him,

4. Made a searching and fearless moral inventory of ourselves.

5. Admitted to God, to ourselves, and to another human being the exact nature of our wrongs.

6. Were entirely ready to have God remove all these defects of character.

7. Humbly asked Him to remove our shortcomings.

8. Made a list of all persons we had harmed, and became willing to make amends to them all.

9. Made direct amends to such people wherever possible, except when to do so would injure them or others.

10. Continued to take personal inventory and when we were wrong promptly admitted it.

11. Sought through prayer and meditation to improve our conscious contact with God as we understood Him, praying only for knowledge of His will for us and the power to carry that out.

12. Having had a spiritual awakening as a result of these steps, we tried to carry this message to alcoholics, and to practice these principles in all our affairs.

In AA's pamphlet, "This is AA" Alcoholics Anonymous makes a statement that I believe is loaded with more deceit than I have ever seen in one sentence; *"There are also atheists and agnostics among us. Belief in, or adherence to, a formal creed is not a condition of membership"*. Yes, you may be an atheist in AA; how else would they get the opportunity to convert you to the AA religion? Yes, you may be of any creed to be in AA; how else would they get the opportunity to convert you to the AA religion? The following is how Alcoholics Anonymous executes their indoctrination and religious conversion.

STEP ONE- The Bait-And-Switch Begins

Step One: We admitted we were powerless over alcohol- that our lives had become unmanageable

In this first foray into the program, AA hides the fact that to complete this Step the prospect must seek God's will.

Upon entering the program, you are presented with the Twelve Steps, and told that no one is going to try to change your religion. After all, AA is not religious. What you are not told is that once you begin working the program, each step evolves into a religious exercise matching or surpassing the religious wording that they told you wasn't actually religious. Step One is changed when you work Step Two; Step Two is changed when you work Step Three... and on and on.

The first step is a prime example, and should serve as an early warning of how Alcoholics Anonymous lures the unexpected into its religion. In order to understand how each Step furthers the indoctrination program it is necessary to constantly look further into AA's written description of their program; if a member wants to know what AA's intent actually is in each Step they need to look several Steps further because AA hides the truth for as long as they can in order to nurse their members along the path to God. Each seemingly innocuous task is progressively weighted with religious purpose until they become nothing more and nothing less than worship of God.

One might ask; "How could anyone have a big problem with this step? How can this be considered religious?" Keep in mind that this program is a graduated indoctrination- one Step leads to another with each Step building on the one before it and, as you progress through those Steps, AA actually changes the instructions in the previous Steps. So it is with Step One; it is later modified to include a mandatory element, a *desire to seek and do God's will*- but they don't reveal that until later. Though AA members are instructed to conceal the religious nature of the program, if you know where to look in AA's writings it becomes clear that while Step One appears to require only a seemingly benign admission to an alcohol problem, it is actually later defined as "seeking God's will". THAT is how Alcoholics Anonymous works; a religious bait-and-switch.

Step One demands that you declare that you cannot manage your own lives, and specifies alcohol as the reason. Looking deeper into the program, you find that AA strives to convince you that only God can solve this problem. Not belief in God, or worship of God, but God Himself. AA gives NO OTHER course of action. Personal strength is banned. Strength of character is ridiculed. Why must we accept powerlessness? -

because in AA no human power can relieve our alcoholism. If we are powerless, and no other human power can help us, what remains? In AA, the answer is God, but they don't disclose that until later after they've had a chance to start the indoctrination process.

AA presents to the novice only that seemingly simple statement — admit you are powerless over alcohol. Not a big red flag — any normal person assumes that this means something along the line of seeking counseling, but Step One is changed as the program progresses to an explicitly religious exercise as AA slowly admits its religious nature. What begins as a simple recognition "*That we were alcoholic and could not manage our own lives*" evolves by Step Seven into an effort to "*to seek and do God's will*" through AA's sneaky use of the word 'humble'. That seemingly innocuous little word is used by AA to change the instructions of Step one after several steps have been worked. In this Step, as in each Step, AA says one thing but means something entirely different.

AA's Step One is a statement that is rife with hidden meaning, a meaning that they don't reveal to the prospect until later, after AA's indoctrination has had time to take hold. AA instructs that "*little good can come to any alcoholic who joins AA unless he has first accepted his devastating weakness and all its consequences. Until he humbles himself, his sobriety- if any- will be precarious. Of real happiness he will find none at all. Proved beyond doubt by an immense experience, this is one of the facts of AA life"*. This is a very illustrative passage in AA literature and points up a big part of the organization's strategy. It's important to note the addition of "humble" there- what exactly do they mean? Here, a good look at the word 'humility' could be helpful.

What is humility and what part does it play in Alcoholics Anonymous? For AA to demand humility of its members should be a good, desirable and even innocuous element of the program. I myself try to be humble in my daily life. As many men my age have, I've finally figured out that my poop does, indeed, stink just as much as everyone else's. When I see a homeless man on the street, I don't look down my nose at them but I realize instead that I'm only a circumstance or two from being in the same boat. I'm in no way better than him, just more fortunate and I am grateful for what good fortune I have. That, to me, is at least some humility and I believe that I possess at least an acceptable level of that quality. When I catch myself getting a little full of myself for any particular reason, I have the self-awareness to give myself a little mental slap upside the head and remember that I am not an exceptional man (and, really, very few men are). I believe that young men enter adulthood ready to conquer the world and from there one of two things happens; they succeed at that goal or they don't. From there, I think that humility comes into play to determine the true quality of that man.

Humility, for a man that does not achieve success, is ironic. If he lacks humility, the failure to achieve the success that he so completely expected will turn into a bitterness which can engulf him. His lack of humility, his inability to accept that he is just like everyone else (as almost everyone is) can lead down only dark paths. If one lacks humility, there comes a tendency to blame the world for his own failure- after all, how can it be HIS fault? He's good enough to conquer the world, right? If that doesn't happen than what could have prevented it? People being unfair to him? His wife holding him back? Kids? His boss? The government? A man who lacks enough humility to accept life as it has played out and accept that his life is what HE made it can become a bitter, twisted wreck. In the best case scenario he just wallows in bitterness. Or, at the other end of the scale, he picks up an AR-15 and strikes out at all of his imagined persecutors. The ironic thing is that most people don't succeed at life as they had hoped they would; the only failure is letting that lack of expected success beat you. A humble man accepts his life and can be content with what he is able to achieve. A humble man accepts what he can do while a man lacking in humility blames others for his failures. That's the irony; humility in failure creates success at being a human being. That, at least, is my view of humility and others may very well define it in a completely different way. Alcoholics Anonymous, however, has a very specific and peculiar definition of humility.

While Merriam-Webster Dictionary defines 'humble' as "not proud or haughty, not arrogant or assertive", Alcoholics Anonymous defines it somewhat differently; as "*a desire to seek and do God's will*". Throughout the steps the words "humility" and "humble" are sprinkled. The common idea of what "humility" and "humble" mean is that you don't feel that you are better than other people – that we are all somewhat alike. This however is not what AA defines as humble. In AA "That basic ingredient of all humility" is "a desire to seek and do God's will". This "desire to seek and do God's will" is specified by AA as "a necessity" to work Step One. This is made clear only when AA feels they have a foothold in the members mind. What was a program of "suggestions" becomes one of "necessities". Due to their policy of graduated indoctrination, this is only revealed as a "necessity" after you are more than halfway through the Twelve Steps. In Step Seven AA clarifies what they actually mean in Step One; after having defined "humble" as a desire to "seek and do God's will" AA declares that "*Every newcomer in Alcoholics Anonymous is told, and soon realizes for himself, that his humble admission of powerlessness over alcohol is his first step toward liberation from its paralyzing grip. So it is that we first see humility as a necessity.*" This is the type of trickery and dishonesty that Alcoholics Anonymous has used to bulk up its membership rolls.

The first Step of Alcoholics Anonymous is a good place to look when you want to understand the ruthless dishonesty with which they treat prospective members. First, they tell the prospect that they are entering a non-religious alcohol treatment program, then they get the prospect to start practicing certain exercises that they call "Steps". After they have practiced these Steps, which AA swore were not religious, AA tells the member that, "Oh, actually, you've been seeking the knowledge of God's will and the strength to carry it out when you worked the Steps. SURPRISE!!" This dishonesty is inherent in every Step of Alcoholics Anonymous, AA declaring that "*the attainment of greater humility*" — the "desire to seek and do God's will" — "*is the foundation principal of each of AA's Twelve Steps. For without some degree of humility*, (again "the desire to seek and do gods will") "*no alcoholic can stay sober at all*".

And so this dishonesty continues in Step Two.

STEP Two- The Savage Atheist and Deadly Sin

<u>2. Came to believe that a Power greater than ourselves could restore us to sanity.</u>

This Step raises chutzpah to a new level. Here they try to tell us that a Higher Power is not religious, but later they tell us that its name is God.

AA, in Steps Two and Three, perpetrates perhaps the most audacious, deliberate and brazen fraud that I have ever seen in my life. This is where Alcohol Anonymous really accelerates the part of their indoctrination in which they lie about the meanings of the words in their doctrine. I don't mean mislead, or distort, or leave parts out; they just flat-out lie. To achieve their end- the religious conversion of those who are not seeking that conversion or who actively don't want that conversion- they must tell a lie here and say that they don't mean God. It is not hard to look further into their texts and find that they do indeed mean God in very unambiguous language but, because their graduated indoctrination relies so heavily on hiding their religion, AA will fight tooth and nail against admitting it. This conflict results in statements by AA that are so ridiculous that this organization's credibility is destroyed. Here, they tell prospects that this "Higher Power" can be anything that the prospect wants it to be, even a chair or the AA group itself. That, however, is a lie.

The reader should ask themselves "What is a Power greater than ourselves?" If there is no exposure to AA's writings, and AA does not have the opportunity to mislead the inductee at their meetings, the answer is obvious; some form of God or supernatural being. This, however, does not suit the needs of Alcoholics Anonymous. AA's single purpose is to convert people to their religion and the method that they've chosen is to present their program as ONLY alcohol treatment and to disavow any religious quality. They have to deny this religious quality even as they are teaching that the ONLY cure for alcoholism is to pray to a Higher Power to cure their alcoholism. That is some trick. I must warn the reader; some of the twists and turns that AA does with the English language, that I will describe in this book, may be severe enough to cause nausea. These semantic tricks are directed towards all but they seem to particularly focus on atheists and agnostics.

In AA's texts, they dedicate large portions to atheists and agnostics. These writings seem to be divided into two main purposes; from one side of AA's mouth we are attacked for our beliefs (such as being called belligerent savages) and from the other side of their mouth we are told that atheism is completely compatible with AA doctrine. Being an atheist I have been verbally attacked my entire life but I have never been as offended as I am by the attacks that are written into the texts of Alcoholics Anonymous. What I find so offensive is the unique combination of condescension, attacks on my beliefs themselves and attacks on my intellect for being an atheist. Its one thing slamming my beliefs but another to tell me that being an atheist means, necessarily, that I am confused and prejudiced. But what puts the insults thrown my way by Alcoholics Anonymous into a level of offensiveness all its own is AA's unmitigated gall of telling me, after ripping me a new one and telling me that my beliefs are just so much nonsense, that my atheism is completely compatible with AA doctrine. The disrespect to my intelligence is breathtaking.

The dilemma faced by AA is that while persuading people to turn to God, they also must pretend that they are not religious. To achieve this, they give explicit lessons to their members on how to hide AA's true nature; the Big Books chapter 'Working With Others' instructs their recruiters that *"you had better use everyday language to describe spiritual principles. There is no use arousing any prejudice he may have against certain theological terms and conceptions about which he may already be confused"*. This approach of concealing the truth is used throughout AA; 'a desire to seek and do God's will' becomes 'humility', 'God' becomes a 'Higher Power', and a confession of the 'Seven Deadly Sins' of Christian teachings becomes 'taking a moral inventory'. By using these terms, AA is able to sow confusion in the minds of prospective members who come to them already in a difficult state of mind, beset by troubles of some sort and being under some degree of mental pressure (possibly *great* pressure). This engineered confusion is furthered by the people outside of Alcoholics Anonymous who, nonetheless, are serving as full partners in this campaign of indoctrination. This is where the cooperation of the alcohol recovery industry and the various tentacles of our justice system come into play.

The nonsense that AA tells prospects about Step Two is so ridiculous that any person of even remotely reasonable intelligence would reject it out of hand but AA has partners, such as alcohol counselors and court officers, that work hard to convince prospects that AA isn't lying; it's just that the prospect doesn't understand what AA is saying and that their disease is causing them to resist their "treatment". The confusion and self-doubt, which this ganging up causes, provides AA that much more time to brainwash the prospect. Their main goal here is just to keep the prospect going to meetings and to keep them listening; they know that the indoctrination won't work if the member sees the truth and walks away, so they try to obscure that truth by telling them that the "Higher Power" AA speaks of is not anything in particular, that you can use anything or anyone as your Higher Power and you'll be able to work the program with no conflict to your religious beliefs; *"You can, if you wish, make AA itself your 'higher power".* It isn't until after you have undergone several more steps of their indoctrination that you are told "Hee Hee, OK, we really do mean God". (It's interesting to note that when the 'Higher Power' is the AA group, it's in lower case. Otherwise, it's upper case).

AA has a problem; how do they try to convince people to turn there will and their lives over to God, but also promote themselves as non-religious? They start by referring to God (at this point) as a "Higher Power". This plays very well into their policy of deception through obfuscation. It allows them to posit a ridiculous assertion that the higher power can be a *chair* and, when the obvious ludicrousness of that is pointed out, to call any doubters of that nonsense belligerent and prejudiced. Their promotion of this so-called logic is spread out over several pages of AA texts, but it should now be thoroughly examined to understand how AA uses chicanery to indoctrinate people into its religion.

This Step is the point at which AA's Big Lie is birthed; that AA's "Power greater than ourselves" is not religious. AA tells prospects that they can use anything as their Higher Power, even the group itself but that lie is simply a way of getting the prospect to set aside their beliefs so AA can replace those beliefs with AA theology.

A major part of AA's indoctrination strategy is to teach about God while denying the religiosity of the program. In order to defend itself from accusations of religiosity they assign twin and diametrically opposed definitions to this theology; AA defines its Higher Power as being anything the member chooses while simultaneously denouncing that definition. While they say in this Step that that Power is anything they want it to be, supernatural or not, in the Big Book chapter "We Agnostics" they explicitly define that power as God; "*...it was impossible for any of us to fully define or comprehend that Power, which is God*". As we can see, while AA tells its members that their own definition of a Higher Power will work fine, in reality AA believes that the only acceptable definition of 'Higher Power' is 'God'. This semantic bait-and-switch is a prime example of the word games that Alcoholics Anonymous is comprised of. Using the lie that praying to a Higher Power is not religious gives them an excuse to attack those who do not share their religion.

A very good illustration of how Alcoholics Anonymous feels towards those who disagree with their religion is on the first page of the chapter dedicated to Step Two in the AA publication 'Twelve Steps and Twelve Traditions' (the 12x12

Book); "*Let's look at the case of the one who says he won't believe- the belligerent one. He is in a state of mind which can be described only as savage*". That is the message from an organization which also claims that atheists should have no problem working their program. The meaning of this is clear; people of all religious persuasions should have no problem in Alcoholics Anonymous as long as they are willing to abandon ALL of their beliefs and accept ALL of the religion of Alcoholics Anonymous. This same message applies to every other religion on earth; AA is not unique in this respect though they try mightily to prove that they are. Just as with any other religion, if you want to be a member of Alcoholics Anonymous you must accept their religious teachings. You can disagree with them and continue going to meetings but that same rule applies to most religions. I don't know of any religion that will bar people from their services simply because they are not of that creed; indeed, just as the case with Alcoholics Anonymous, they would welcome the opportunity of converting them. While I don't mean this book to be about the conflict between atheism and the religion of Alcoholics Anonymous I do feel that that AA's attack on atheists, so prominently pursued in AA literature, provides a very clear window into AA's indoctrination process. It helps that Alcoholics Anonymous has written about their opinions, and hate, towards atheists so thoroughly.

In the Twelve Steps and Twelve Traditions book, and in the "Alcoholics Anonymous" chapter "We Agnostics" (which AA refers to as the "Big Book"), AA makes clear their attitude towards atheism, agnosticism and any other religious belief that conflicts with Alcoholic Anonymous religion; those other beliefs are wrong, belligerent and savage philosophies which are only lightly held by their adherents ("...*cheer up, something like half of us thought we were atheists or agnostics*"). To AA, we only *thought* we were atheists. Those adherents of other religions are simply closed- minded and they will see the AA light once they stop fighting and start practicing AA religion enthusiastically. Of course, such dismissive disdain is not solely directed at atheists. For those who once were churchgoers, but now reject that theology, AA refers to their beliefs as indifference, fancied self-sufficiency, prejudice and defiance. In Alcoholics Anonymous, all religions are welcome as long as their adherents realize how wrong they are. Now AA's task is to convert them and show them the only true path; the religious teachings of AA. The tool that AA chose to achieve that conversion is deceit.

In the chapter "Working With Others" in the Big Book, AA instructs sponsors to not use clear language when discussing the religious principles of

AA. It directs them to use "everyday language" to discuss AA's religious principles. They write that this is to avoid any "prejudices" the prospect may have against certain theological terms about which he may already be "confused" about. AA stresses the need to refer to God as a "Higher Power" of one's own conception. This is clearly reflective of AA philosophy; if you are not religious, you are "prejudiced" and if you would disagree with AA religion, than you are confused.

Having assured the prospect that they may work Step Two no matter what their religious persuasion is, while hiding the fact that they are on a path which leads only to God, AA now introduces that God in Step Three.

STEP Three- Genetic Memory Of God

<u>Step Three: Made a decision to turn our will and our lives over to God as we understood him.</u>

This Step envisions that the prospect is far along enough in their indoctrination to actually call AA's deity God, but still protects its fraud with the phrase "as we understand Him". While slamming self-will and self-sufficiency, they blame all of the world's ills on its occupants not worshipping as AA members do.

In this Step, AA continues their indoctrinative strategy of hiding the program's religiosity by making up false meanings for the religious elements that they are trying to shield from questioning; they keep prospects on the hook by telling them that when they say God, they don't mean God. The chapter dedicated to this Step in 'Twelve Steps and Twelve Traditions' shows them building on the deceit that AA introduced in Step Two when AA jumped through hoops to assure them that they could use anything as a Higher Power, even the AA group itself.. *Now* AA defines that as "faith", a decidedly religious exercise. This is symptomatic of AA's graduated indoctrination; they instruct prospects to do something, and then change the very character of that task once they've had time to brainwash them. That's AA's trick; by causing the prospect to have doubt, they have managed to keep them coming back. If they're not in some sort of in-patient rehab, and they attend the amount of meetings that they tell them to attend, they've been allowed several hours per week to drive their message into the prospects head. If they are in a rehab, then they have had access to them 24 hours per day, seven days a week. They use that time to gradually introduce their faith-healing religion into the prospect's mind and slowly convert a normal person into a person who believes that disease can, and will, be cured by prayer.

In the immediately previous Step, Step Two, AA convinced the prospect to turn their will and lives over to a Higher Power. They claimed that this wasn't religious, that the Higher Power could be anything the prospect desired- including the AA group. But what is the prospect supposed to make of that? The most reasonable interpretation, at least from a normal person's perspective, is to seek guidance from the group. That, however, is circular reasoning. AA is claiming that the prospect is not learning religion but dictates that if they don't believe in God, the answer is solved by taking guidance from a group that wants you to turn your will and life over to God. Another solution is offered in group meetings is to use a chair as your Higher Power. Assuming the speaker was sane, what does that mean? Unless they actually attribute supernatural powers to inanimate objects, the only conclusion that I can come to is that they are speaking about meditation. Even if that is true it is still part of AA deception because, later in the Steps, they explicitly warn against such relying on any guidance received through meditation. In Step Five Alcoholics Anonymous dictates that you must make sure that your guidance in AA comes directly from God- not somebody else, not yourself, only from the mouth of God to your ears.

According to AA if we talk to a chair, or anyone or anything else, we may consider that our Higher Power. In this Step that Higher Power is changed; no longer is it anything we choose but is now called God. While we are going through the program, this seems to be simply a subtle and unimportant shift; simply a change in the words we are using- no big deal. But if we look at what has transpired, then the graduated indoctrination strategy of Alcoholics Anonymous comes into somewhat clearer focus. A review of what has passed would be helpful to that focus.

When we entered AA, we were told that the program is not religious and we were simply asked to admit we have an alcohol problem (our lives are unmanageable). Then we were told that we need a Higher Power to help us solve our problem but we were assured that that can be anything we choose- the group, our mother, a chair. Now we are told that that Higher Power- SURPRISE! - is actually God.

This is what AA does; they get you to practice their religion by telling you that it's not religion. They later tell you that, actually, it was AA religion and because you participated they say that that proves you share AA's religious beliefs and you've just been fooling yourself your entire life. This logic is revealed by AA in their Big Book chapter "We Agnostics"; "*Actually, we were fooling ourselves, for deep down in every man, woman, and child, is the fundamental idea of God. It may be obscured by calamity, by pomp, by worship of other things, but in some form or other it is there. For faith in a Power greater than ourselves, and miraculous demonstrations for that power in human lives, are facts as old as man himself*".

We have proceeded to go from not practicing religion (or practicing a religion different from the faith-healing of Alcoholics Anonymous) to turning our lives over to God. Could it be that someone is fibbing to us? Could they really be trying to get us to worship God? One thing is clear; AA is trying to trick us into joining their religious services by pretending that the program is not religious. This Step will bring us that much closer to worshiping their God and joining them in their faith-healing rituals by getting us to accept that we are now, and have always been, worshipping God. AA, though, is not yet ready to admit where it is leading its followers; they still need to nurse their members' God-conscience along until it takes a firmer hold.

This Step focuses on a big part of the Alcoholics Anonymous process of indoctrination, the phrase "God as we understand Him". Alcoholics Anonymous has relied for decades, and continues to rely, on this qualification to shield itself from the scrutiny. Having stealthily altered the "Higher Power" to "God", they had to find a way to continue their hard and fast policy of denying the religiosity of their program even as they tell the prospect to worship God. That is why AA adds the phrase "as we understand Him". Of course, they don't reveal until much later that the program is designed to help their members "*better understand Him*" until they learn to "*love God, and call Him by name*".

The question at the core of whether Alcoholics Anonymous is telling the truth about whether or not a person can work the AA program without worshipping God is answered in this Step. It is in this Step that AA so strongly reveals that it has been lying about AA not being religious. Still, they manage to camouflage the truth about AA religion as well as can be done while desperately working the "not religious" lie into books which strive to convert people into fundamentalist, faith-healing God worshippers while simultaneously convincing them that AA's program is secular.

Because of that herculean effort at obfuscation, it helps to use the two main texts of Alcoholics Anonymous- 'The Big Book' and 'Twelve Steps and Twelve Traditions' (the 12x12) when getting at the truth.

Looking at the chapter in 12x12 dedicated to Step Three, certain phrases and words are introduced which, though seemingly rather benign and unimportant, AA has loaded with religious significance. The first word that comes into prominence is "willingness". This is actually an excellent example of AA's stated policy of using everyday words to disguise theological concepts in order to confuse the prospect into submission and conversion. A simple word like 'willingness" is used by Alcoholics Anonymous to convince the non-believer (or other-believer) that, though he may have thought that he didn't believe in AA's faith-healing, he actually has believed that way his entire life. 'Willingness' is described in Step Three as the 'key' to this Step, but what is 'willingness'? As AA uses it, it is another tool to increase the religiosity of the Steps that their members have already completed. That is the essence of AA indoctrination; they tell members to perform religious rituals while they are assured that these activities are not religious. Once they have completed them, AA then tells them that, actually, they were worshipping God. In their logic, that is a reason that anyone can work the Steps without being religious; once AA tricks a person into performing a religious ritual, that proves that the tricked person is actually religious but was just in denial. In this Step, AA redefines what we did in Step Two when we adopted the group as our 'Higher Power'. Now AA tells us that what we *actually* did was turn our wills and our lives over to <u>*divine*</u> guidance.

In Step Two AA told us that we could, even as atheists, use the group as a Higher Power non-religiously. Now, in Step Three, in order to show us that we can turn our lives over to God, AA redefines what we did in Step Two as "*faith*" and tells us that "*Every man and woman who has joined AA and intends to stick has, without realizing it, made a beginning on Step Three. Isn't it true that in all matters touching upon alcohol, each of them has decided to turn his or her life over to the care, protection and guidance of Alcoholics Anonymous? Already a willingness has been achieved to cast out one's own will and one's own ideas about the alcohol problem in favor of those suggested by AA. Any willing newcomer feels sure AA is the only safe harbor for the foundering vessel he has become. Now if this is not turning one's will and life over to a newfound Providence, then what is it?*" Again, Alcoholics Anonymous practices the religious indoctrination bait-and-switch while giving us a new word-of-the-day; 'willing (ness)'.

'Willingness' is described by AA as key to this Step but, again, what does AA mean by 'willingness'? We should keep in mind that AA believes that everyone on the face of the earth, for all of time, shares their religious beliefs and that those who say that they don't are just "fooling themselves". AA declares *the effectiveness of the whole AA program will rest upon how well and earnestly we have tried to come to a decision to turn our will and our lives over to the care of God as we understand Him*" (Notice the capitalization). Towards that end, AA declares in 12x12 that for Step Three *there is only one key, and it is called willingness"* and provides instructions and examples of what they are actually speaking of when they say "willing".

In the We Agnostics chapter of the Big Book, they discuss "willingness". They write of working with atheists and agnostics and how the prospect's hope would rise until AAers began to speak of God. The AAers would commiserate with the atheist because they have shared his "*doubt and prejudice"* and the 'Big Book' helpfully explains how, as atheists, we could not understand our own beliefs. In keeping with AA doctrine which holds that all atheists are just in denial- that belief in God is an innate part of our genetic makeup- AA tells us that atheists find themselves "*thinking, when enchanted by a starlit night, Who then made all this?*" AA declares that atheists and agnostics can work this religious program thusly; "*...as soon as we are able to lay aside prejudice and express even a willingness to be believe in a Power greater than ourselves, we commenced to get results, even though it was impossible for any of us to fully define or comprehend that Power, which is God*". This is 'willingness' in AA; Alcoholics Anonymous doctrine holds that people who don't believe in faith-healing should have no problem working this program as long as they are *willing* to abandon their beliefs and convert to AA religion.

AA is able to behave in the manner that they do because of one core belief they have; all people, whether they know it or not, believe in God. They believe that we are born with this belief and if we think that we are atheist or agnostic we are in denial. When AA cooperates with one of our government agencies, or alcohol rehabs, in reporting attendance at their services, via attendance sheet signing, they believe that they are just getting us to know the truth; the religion of Alcoholics Anonymous. They believe that they just have to keep hammering at us until we become willing to believe.

It's also in Step Three that Alcoholics Anonymous begins its assault on the concepts of intellectual independence, self- determination and self-sufficiency in both alcoholics and non-alcoholics. In order to bolster these attacks, AA folds language in on itself by declaring that the more dependent people become on a Higher Power (as always, capitalized) the more independent that they actually are. To this end, they attempt to equate reliance on God to a reliance on electricity.

In the 12x12 book, in Step Three, AA compares relying on God to relying on electricity. They declare that when we depend on electricity and the great benefits that electricity provides-power and light- we become independent, comfortable and secure. They refer to electricity as *"that strange energy so few people understand"* that meets our simplest and most desperate needs. They cite the *"polio sufferer confined to an iron lung who depends with complete trust upon a motor to keep the breath of life in him"*. AA posits that as an analogy to reliance on God and, in doing so, denounces personal self-determination and a reliance on intellect; *"But the moment our mental or emotional independence is in question, how differently we behave. How persistently we claim the right to decide all by ourselves just what we shall think and just how we shall act... all of the decisions are to be ours alone... We are certain that our intelligence, backed by willpower, can rightly control our inner lives... This brave philosophy, wherein each man plays God, sounds good in the speaking, but it still has to meet the acid test; how well does it actually work"*. Of course, the analogy that this is all based on is demonstrably faulty. Electricity is not a "strange energy"; in can be measured and quantified, physically felt and sensed and is thoroughly understood by hundreds of millions. It is generated and does actual physical work (or more precisely, is converted to actual work). I don't have "faith" in electricity, for it can fail. I must purchase it because it is derived from energy sources and converted into its useful form. The only similarity, in my opinion, is that both electricity and AA religion are generated by people rather than a deity. Of course, no one should operate under the delusion that Alcoholics Anonymous actually believes that analogy; it is just another word game that AA plays, hoping that their target audience is unable to see beyond simple semantic facades. It's nothing more than a manipulation of words meant to provide a jumping-off point for an attack on free-thought and self-determination outside of religion. This focused attempt to denounce self-will and self-determination isn't simply an element of the program; it is an intensification of the indoctrination process aimed at moving the prospect to the God-consciousness described at the end of Step Three in the 12x12 Book. Making the case for why Alcoholics Anonymous is right and everyone else in the world is wrong, AA answers that question, *"how well does it actually work"* with a full-throated attack on those who don't believe in AA theology, blaming all of the world's woes on those who don't think as AA dictates that they should. Speaking of alcoholics who believes in self-sufficiency; *"Should his own image in the mirror be too awful to contemplate (and it usually is), he might first take a look at the results normal people are getting from self-sufficiency. Everywhere he sees people filled with anger and fear, society breaking up into warring fragments. Each fragment says to the others 'We are right and you are wrong'. Every such pressure group, if it is strong enough, self -righteously imposes it's will upon the rest. And everywhere the same thing is being done on an individual basis. The sum of all this mighty effort is less peace and less brotherhood than before. The philosophy of self-sufficiency is not paying off. Plainly enough, it is a bone-crushing juggernaut whose final achievement is in ruin."* While declaring that the Twelve Steps are not religious, Alcoholics Anonymous denounces free thought, only allowing a person to act in accordance with divine guidance. That hypocrisy would be bad enough if the criticism of personal freedom were confined to discussions of alcoholics' behavior, but AA denounces un-Godly thinking for *everyone.* We all live in *"bone crushing juggernaut whose final achievement is ruin"* because the whole world doesn't practice the religion of Alcoholics Anonymous.

In the final two paragraphs of Step Three in the 12x12 Book AA makes clear what they have been steering the prospect to. While denouncing free thought and self-determination AA describes what a good and proper member of Alcoholics Anonymous should believe, assuming they have obeyed AA so far, as well as what is wrong with our religious beliefs. They tell us that "*Our whole trouble had been the misuse of willpower. We had tried to bombard our problems with it instead of attempting to bring it into agreement with God's intention for us*" To fix that, Alcoholics Anonymous tells us that "*when try to make our will conform with God's that we begin to use it rightly*"
. Only when the member agrees with these terms may they practice Step Three; "*Thy will be done, not mine*".

STEP Four- The Seven Deadly Sins

<u>Step Four: Made a searching and fearless moral inventory of ourselves.</u>

AA's "moral inventory" is put forth by AA as non-religious, and it certainly sounds like a wonderful thing, but in AA you can't take anything at face value. In reality it is an exploration of how far "we depart from... God".

A very good indication as to where Alcoholics Anonymous has steered their members' minds is the very first word in the chapter on Step Four; Creation. It's also a symptom of the deceit of AA; while pretending that it isn't religious, AA adheres to the biblical story of Creation. It is also a good peek at how seemingly rational and benign statements like Step Four, taking a moral inventory, are actually religion masquerading as reason. This Step is, in reality, an examination of *"the point at which we depart from the degree of perfection that God wishes for us..."* This Step is all about Sin, as defined in the Bible.

Alcoholics Anonymous, as is its norm, uses this simple phrase- a moral inventory- to inculcate in us ancient Christian theology. AA gives several terms that different groups of people might use when speaking of a 'moral inventory' before specifying that, for Alcoholics Anonymous, it is an inventory of how we have committed the Seven Deadly Sins.

"To avoid falling into confusion over the names these defects should be called, let's take a universally recognized list of major human failings- the Seven Deadly Sins of pride, greed, lust, anger, gluttony, envy, and sloth". There is the typical AA arrogance in this statement; by terming this Christian list as "universally recognized", they imbue their religion with universal acceptance and assert that their religious beliefs are accepted by all people of the earth. This keys into, and reinforces, their arrogant belief that everyone is born with a belief in God and that a refusal to worship God is a mental liability. Alcoholics Anonymous thus becomes nothing more, and nothing less, than a radical Christian sect which bases its theology on a version of the Seven Deadly Sins. Their entire program is a process of its members' searching their souls for the Seven Deadly Sins of Christian theology that they have committed and the Steps they take to correct, and atone for, those Sins.

The faith-healing doctrine of AA is specific and unique to AA. While Alcoholics Anonymous promotes itself as not conflicting with other religious beliefs, that is false. While incorporating the Sin concept of Christianity, their method of dealing with that sin is specific to the religion of Alcoholics Anonymous.

The Seven Deadly Sins (source; Wikipedia) are hardcore Christian teachings and are taught by both the Catholic and Christian churches. The Seven Deadly Sins, also known as the capital vices or cardinal sins, is a classification of objectionable vices (part of Christian ethics) that have been used since early Christian times to educate and instruct Christians concerning fallen humanity's tendency to sin. In the Catholic Church, such sins have specific rituals, such as Confession with a priest. AA teaches in Step Five (the next Step) that that is unnecessary, that it can simply be any other human being. But, of course, AA tells us that they have nothing to do with religion. That is shown in this Step to be so far from the truth as to be laughable. Catholics believe in confession to a priest while Alcoholics Anonymous doesn't; while a catholic could do both, is it morally acceptable for the courts and substance abuse professionals to require Catholics to learn religious rituals that run counter to their church's teachings? Is it right to force a Muslim to accept Christian teachings on the Seven Deadly Sins? Are the human rights violations committed against these, and others', freedom of conscience acceptable in a free society?

Alcoholics Anonymous bases their reasoning for faith-healing as a cure for alcoholism on a very straight-forward principle; alcoholism is caused by the Seven Deadly Sins. In their discussion of conducting a moral inventory, they are directing us to see how we have committed the

Seven Deadly Sins. It is at the heart of AA theology that alcoholism is a direct result of sinning, citing that as the "primary" reason for alcoholism and failure at life. That is the purpose of taking a moral inventory, for AA members to discover how they have sinned their way to alcoholism. However, in its obsessive need to present itself as not being a religion, AA wants to have its cake and eat it to; though they've defined the 'character defects' of this Step as the Seven Deadly Sins, they attempt to bury the religiosity of this Step through a progressive use of synonyms for those defects, for those Seven Deadly Sins. Upon close examination of how AA evolves its language, the deep Christian fervor of this Step (and of the AA program) can be further brought to light.

AA begins the chapter for Step Four by speaking of instincts and declares them bestowed by a Creator, also referring to these instincts as 'desires'. AA explains that *"Creation gave us instincts for a purpose. So these desires... are perfectly necessary and right, and surely God-given..."* However, *"these instincts... often exceed their proper functions... When that happens... the instincts... have turned to liabilities."* AA thus creates three synonyms for the same thing (which they consider were given to us by God during the biblical event of Creation); instincts, desires, and once they get out of hand, liabilities. It is here that

AA prepares for the transition from referring to these things as liabilities to using a term that becomes important in the coming Step Six; 'character defects'.

AA defines Step Four as *"our vigorous and painstaking effort to discover what these liabilities in each of us had been, and are"* and explains that these instincts run wild- these *liabilities*- are what caused our drinking, AA revealing that *"Alcoholics should be able to see that instincts run wild in themselves is the underlying cause of their destructive drinking".* AA then expounds on the 'moral inventory' that they mandate as part of their program, giving various reasons why some AAers abhor such an inventory. That is stage at where *"...our sponsors come to the rescue... by showing ... that his character defects are not more numerous or worse than those of anyone else in AA".* Hence, AA expands their list of synonyms for the 'Sin' to include *'character defects',* which they will now morph to *'personality defects'* and, in conclusion, gather all of these synonyms together under their true AA definition; *"Seven Deadly Sins".*

As AA progressed through this Step's chapter in the 12x12 Book, we saw them work their way to making the point that these desires become Sins at a certain point and triggered its members' alcoholism. Here again, however, AA goes beyond alcoholics to declare that their theology applies to everyone in the entire world; in the opinion of Alcoholics Anonymous *"Nearly every serious emotional problem can be seen as a case of misdirected instinct. When that happens, our great natural assets, the instincts, have turned into physical and mental liabilities""*. This is an important point in understanding the nature, and goals, of AA. Alcoholics Anonymous is a faith-healing sect of Christianity. They view every emotional problem as stemming from "misdirected instinct"- AA's synonym for the Seven Deadly Sins of Christian theology- and they prescribe turning your will and your life over to God as a cure for every serious emotional problem in the world. When AA tells its members to take a "moral inventory" they are demanding a ritual of which its true religious end purpose is not revealed until Step Six. In that Step, AA defines the character defect that we are searching for as *"the point at which we depart from the degree of perfection that God wishes for us here on earth"*.

AA doesn't simply view this Step as trying to improve ourselves or owning up to the things that we have done wrong in life. They use this Step to enforce fundamentalist Christian theology on its members. This program is linear; you can't proceed to the Step Five before this Step, Step Four. In order to complete this Step members have to conduct a thorough self- examination of how the member has

committed the Seven Deadly Sins of Christian
biblical teachings. To reinforce the mandatory
nature of each Step, for this Step AA declares that
"*...unless he is willing to work hard at the
elimination of the worst of these defects, both
sobriety and peace of mind will still elude him*".
While claiming to be a program of non-religious
'suggestions', AA reveals itself to <u>require</u> the
member pray to have his Seven Deadly Sins
forgiven. If not, the cause of his alcoholism cannot
be removed.

Having identified character defects and
runaway instincts/desires as actually being a
committing of the Seven Deadly Sins, AA declares
that committing those sins is the cause of
alcoholism; "*By now the newcomer has probably
arrived at the following conclusions: that his
character defects, representing instincts gone
astray, have been the primary cause of his drinking
and his failure at life*". AA goes on to declare that
the elimination of those Sins is the only answer for
alcoholism. This Step precedes Steps Five and Six
which are processes of confessions to God and the
prayer to God to help them stop Sinning. AA
concludes this Chapter by revisiting their well-used
word, 'willingness'.

In Step Three, and the Big Book chapter
'We Agnostics', we saw AA's definition of the
word "willing"; the abandonment of one's personal

beliefs and acceptance of AA's faith-healing Christian theology. AA, exploiting that 'willingness', has now submersed their members in Christian teachings of Deadly Sin and have prepared those members to begin their process of Confession and Atonement. Of course, the dear reader might still be willing to cut AA some slack and ask themselves "Is that such a bad thing?". I might agree if not for the problems that this book is aimed at addressing; Alcoholics Anonymous hides all of this and cooperates with people being forced into their religious program. While my successful lawsuit did establish the legal principal that forced AA is unconstitutional, the reach of that ruling was limited because the Supreme Court refused to hear the case. This limited the jurisdiction of the ruling to the area covered by the ruling judicial body. The threat to people's freedom is great. My personal experience gives a window to that threat.

Alcoholics Anonymous, through their professional and legal partners, has the ability to destroy the lives of those who reject the religion of Alcoholics Anonymous. I know that anyone who comes under the purview of AA may be imprisoned in an insane asylum or prison for rejecting AA theology because these were the threats that were leveled against me. Sentenced to three years' probation following a DWI conviction, I was required to attend Alcoholics Anonymous 3 times weekly and participate in an alcohol recovery program. This program, like virtually all others, simply worked hand-in-hand with Alcoholics Anonymous to teach the Twelve Steps and these three entities- probation, my treatment clinic and Alcoholics Anonymous- worked mightily to instill in me this faith-healing religion. When I rejected Alcoholism Anonymous as the religious hokum that it is, I was threatened with imprisonment in both prison and a locked insane asylum. If I did not go to meetings and recite, verbatim, Twelve Step religious teachings in the presence of my probation officer, he could violate my probation and imprison me. When I made clear to the counselors at the treatment facility that I rejected AA teachings, I was told that if I didn't work the Steps they would have me committed to a locked mental health facility. This is the damage that the lies of Alcoholics Anonymous inflicts on freedom of conscience; if some Americans don't learn and love these fundamentalist Christian teachings, they may be incarcerated or committed to insane asylums. Be we Christian, Muslim, Atheist or something else, I believe we need to ask ourselves if this forced religion is what we want in our world.

STEP Five- AA, The Arbiter of God's Word

Step Five; Admitted to God, to ourselves, and to another human being the exact nature of our wrongs.

This is the Step that most concretely marks the end of AA's ability to deny its intensely religious, faith-healing beliefs and where AA makes clear that they view themselves as the only true religion. It is also a means to practice the Christian concept of being forgiven for our Sins. AA tells us that *"This vital Step was also the means by which we began to get the feeling that we could be forgiven, no matter what we had thought or done"*.

In the previous Step Alcoholics Anonymous made it clear that, in their view, alcoholism is the direct result of committing the Seven Deadly Sins. In this Step, AA warns us that *"scarcely any Step is more necessary to longtime sobriety and peace of mind than this one"* because *"It seems plain that the grace of God will not enter to expel our destructive obsessions until we are willing to try this"*. Having previously made clear that, in their doctrine, a belief in God is inherent in every human in history, and that alcoholism is the direct result of Biblical Sin, AA now declares that for an alcoholic, this Biblical Sin cannot be atoned for without the religion of the AA's Fifth Step. If you wish to seek the grace of God, AA's Step Five is the only answer. However, if you challenge an acolyte of AA on this, the same old defenses are always presented; "It's God *as we understand Him*", "They're only suggestions", "Everyone's welcome in AA", "It's spiritual, not religious". In this Step, however, AA puts lie to all of that and makes clear that their program requires contact with the God of the Bible.

Can "God" in AA be anything we choose? In Step Five that becomes impossible — the protestations of non-religiosity stop. Here, God is a non-human entity that speaks to us. We are specifically instructed that the words that come from inside ourselves are not good enough; only words *verified* as coming from God's can be trusted. This step makes it impossible for God to be anything except a supernatural being. The prospect now has a choice; pray to a supernatural power or abandon the program. If he is under threat of imprisonment the choice is this; live his life in a jail cell or bow down before a God he doesn't believe in.

AA declares that Step Five is "*the beginning of a true kinship with God*" and makes clear that that God is a supernatural being, referring to that God using Christian terminology. Whereas AA had promised us that we would be able to use anything we want as a Higher Power, and that God would be "as we understand Him", in this Step AA explicitly bars us from relying on our own understanding of what God tells us. AA doesn't simply want members to have a relationship with God; they want members to talk to God, hear back from Him and then have His words verified as coming truly from God. That is the reasoning behind having us confess our Seven Deadly Sins to God and another human being, so that our interpretation of God's will is acceptable to Alcoholics Anonymous.

AA, while they deny religiosity, tells us that many members have qualms with this Step, crying out; *"Why can't God as we understand Him tell us where we went astray? If the Creator gave us our lives in the first place...Why don't we make our admissions to Him directly? Why do we need to bring anyone else into this?"* AA warns against this because *"what comes to us alone may be garbled by our own rationalization and wishful thinking".* While posing as accepting to other religious beliefs, AA makes clear that they are the arbiters of what comes from God and what doesn't; *"How many times have we heard well-intentioned people claim the guidance of God when it was all too plain that they were sorely mistaken?"* This is an extension of AA's arrogance that I have cited elsewhere in this book; AA believes that they know the will and mind of God. While I am no theologian this would seem, to me, to be blasphemy. Who is AA to speak for God? Who is AA to tell me whether the guidance I receive from God is acceptable? Who is AA to mediate for God?

While I believe that AA's secret indoctrination should be offensive to just about anyone that believes in freedom of conscience, AA's condescension towards Atheists and Agnostics is particularly irksome. Many religions on earth share certain similarities, so the differences that people of non-AA religions have with AA will vary. The differences between AA and Atheists, however, are vast and deep. As I wrote earlier, I find it incredibly arrogant that AA helps force their teachings- that every person in history has believed in God and the ones who don't worship God are just in denial- on Atheists. That condescension is what they use to conclude the 12x12 chapter on Step Five; "*Many an AA, once agnostic or atheist, tells us that it was during this stage of Step Five that he first actually felt the presence of God*". That arrogance is, however, not limited to atheists and agnostics.

AA sees itself as the only true religion. They view the religion of AA as one that you must recognize as true, else you are fooling yourself. AA has built itself into the behemoth it is by using one lie; that AA is compatible with all religious beliefs. AA's instructions for this Step get a little closer to the truth; "*even those who had faith already often become conscious of God as they never were before*". Translation: "You may have felt that you religion was good, but AA religion is better- we're closer to God than all those other religions".

STEP Six- We're Men, You're All Boys

Step Six: Were entirely ready to have God remove all these defects of character

It is in this Step that AA makes clear that those who don't believe in a living God are men, and those that choose the "God as we understand Him" that AA lures people in with are boys.

Remembering that Alcoholics Anonymous defines 'character defects' as the Seven Deadly Sins of Christian teachings helps one to grasp the full meaning of Step Six. In this Step, AA pulls together the theological concepts that it has attempted to imbed in the members psyche without that members understanding of what AA was actually doing. In this Step, AA unequivocally declares that the Twelve Steps of Alcoholics Anonymous cures alcoholism with a miracle.

Alcoholics Anonymous is a faith-healing religion. In this Step AA finally declares that its program directs God to cure the alcoholic of his medically recognized disease, and that God obeys. In Step Six of the 12x12 Book, AA tells us *"Of course, the often disputed question of whether God can- and will- remove defects of character ..."* (the Seven Deadly Sins) *"...will be answered with a prompt affirmative by almost any member. He will usually offer his proof in a statement like this... I was beaten, absolutely licked. My own willpower just wouldn't work on alcohol...no human being could do the job for me...But when I...asked a Higher Power, God as I understood Him, to give me release, my obsession to drink vanished. It was lifted right out of me."* This is not meant colloquially, or tongue in cheek, or in any way that makes it so anyone can simply work it into their own belief system. In order to work the Twelve Steps of Alcoholics Anonymous, you must completely embrace faith-healing. AA declares that faith-healing is a fact.

While AA goes to great lengths in its public relations protocols to communicate that, though they use many religious terms, anyone with any beliefs can work their program successfully. When a painstaking look at the passages buried in their texts, the passages that their public relations protocols are designed to hide from the unsuspecting public, is conducted it becomes clear that participation in AA has only one goal; a cure by miracle. In the Big Book chapter 'There Is A Solution', Alcoholics Anonymous lays out, in clear and unambiguous terms, their miracle of healing; *"The great fact.."*- not a 'suggestion', not 'as we understand it', but a *FACT- "...is just this, and nothing less: That we have had deep and effective spiritual experiences which have revolutionized our whole attitude towards life, toward our fellows and toward God's universe. The central fact of our lives today is the absolute certainty that our Creator has entered into our hearts and lives in a way which is indeed miraculous"* Alcoholics Anonymous considers it a FACT- not a suggestion, as their PR pamphlets like to tell people- that the AA program's purpose is to have the Creator enter it's member's lives and perform a miracle. That is faith-healing and to hide that is unethical, which is perhaps the most delicious irony that anyone could ever think up. While rehabilitating people, we teach them to lie and break the law.

When someone breaks the law, we in America take different approaches. In most cases, at least some of our judicial responses to the law-breaker are rehabilitative. In the case of drug and alcohol offenses, rehabilitation and treatment occupy the monster's share of our legal remedies to these offenses. The idea is, of course, to change the offender so that he or she becomes as upstanding, honest and law-abiding citizen. By utilizing Alcoholics Anonymous, we teach the target of our rehabilitation efforts two things; that we approve of lying and deceit and, because forced AA is illegal, we approve of breaking the law. If a person really understands what is going on in Alcoholics Anonymous, we are teaching that anything goes as long as we get what we want. In my case, the probation department and the alcohol rehab wanted me to be a good AA Christian, and they were happy to lie to me, threaten me and violate the United States Constitution- our highest laws- to get what they wanted. What, exactly, should I learn from that? If I truly understand what is being said to me in Alcoholics Anonymous, I learn to lie. While AA members tell the newcomer that AA is not a religious program, they actually know that the program has turned them into faith-healing Christians who believe that it is a FACT that a "Creator" has entered into their lives in a miraculous way. They follow the written instructions of AA, however, and hide that knowledge from the new member and in turn teach that new member to lie. That, in AA, is being a good Christian. Even more, it makes them 'Men' because until you become AA's version of a good Christian, you are a 'boy'.

To Alcoholics Anonymous, this Step is of great importance. It is here that the member becomes a "man"- to AA, a requirement of manhood is to obey God. Only upon acceptance of that do you graduate from 'boy' to 'man'. *"This is the Step that separates the men from the boys. So declares a well-loved clergyman who happens to be one of AA's greatest friends. He goes on to explain that any person capable of enough willingness and honesty to try repeatedly Step Six on all his faults- without any reservations whatsoever- has indeed come a long way spiritually, and is therefore entitle to be called a man who is sincerely trying to grow in the image and likeness of his Creator"* That is put more bluntly further in the chapter; *"So the difference between the boys and the men is the difference between striving for a self-determined objective and for the perfect objective which is of God"*. This chapter makes clear what Alcoholics Anonymous has tried so hard to hide from the public; in AA, Atheists (and those who don't believe exactly as AA does) are BOYS while those who practice the religion of Alcoholics Anonymous are MEN.

STEP Seven- Take My Sin- Please
(my apologies to the Great Mr. Youngman)

<u>Step Seven: Humbly asked Him to remove our shortcomings</u>.

In this Step Alcoholics Anonymous, which so stridently pleads secularism, directs its members to beg God to remove the Seven Deadly Sins from their souls.

Alcoholics Anonymous advertises itself as non-religious and as a program of suggestions rather than mandates. The 12x12 Book's chapter on Step Seven, however, explicitly *requires* actions of the member, citing 'necessities', and continues to drop the guise of non-religiosity in favor of language so steeped in religion that one must conclude that AA is no longer trying to hide their true, faith-healing nature. They are treating AA inductees as one would a standard shift car.

Anyone experienced with driving a stick shift knows that you ease the clutch out as the fuel takes over to get the car moving. This is what AA is doing with the minds of unsuspecting prospects. When the car is at a standstill the clutch pedal is completely depressed (the prospect still believes that AA is medicine rather than faith-healing) and AA has not yet applied the gas (religion). To get the car moving, AA lets the clutch out (they start dropping the non-religious pretense) a little and applies the gas (religion) a little bit. As the car picks up speed (as the indoctrination takes hold) the clutch (pretense) continues to be eased and the gas (religion) is increased. That is continued until the clutch pedal is completely released (no more pretending that they are non-religious) and the gas (religion) is at full throttle. That is where Step Seven gets us to; the pretense has been dropped and the member is cruising down the Holy Highway of AA Salvation and the only thing left is to finish moving through the rest of the gears (Steps) until the member is cruising down the Lord's Freeway at full speed with the winds of salvation blowing back their hair. The problem is that people are not cars; cars are tools and to treat people who at their most vulnerable as nothing more than targets for religious conversion is cruel. The fact that they are unwilling and unaware of what Alcoholics Anonymous is doing makes it despicable and, when AA joins forces with the state to compel this conversion, it is illegal.

While much of the pretense of religiosity has been dropped by this point, AA never ceases their explicitly stated policy of using everyday words to disguise theological concepts. They must, however, indoctrinate members in their religion so they can't totally avoid saying what they truly mean. The tactic is on display, bright as day, in Step Seven's discussion on 'humility'.

Step Seven in the 12x12 Book focuses on the subject of humility,; "*this Step specifically concerns itself with humility...the attainment of greater humility is the foundation principal of each of AA's Twelve Steps. For without some degree of humility, no alcoholic can stay sober at all.*" AA feels so strongly about this quality that it is mentioned in this chapter (in the forms humility, humble and humbly) 33 times over the course of seven pages and 70 times in the book. Of all of those times, only *once* do they reveal what they actually mean when they use that word; "*as long as we placed self-reliance first, a genuine reliance on a higher power was out of the question. That basic ingredient of humility, a desire to seek and do God's will, was missing*". This is how Alcoholics Anonymous indoctrinates people; using their stated policy of camouflaging the deeply religious teachings of AA, they get people to practice the rituals without knowing that they are participating in faith-healing religion; the AA member is told to practice 'humility' but they are not told that in, AA, humility is "*a desire to seek and do God's will*". If the member has the advantage of it being pointed out to them as my book does, the AA inductee can understand what he or she is being told. However, if all they have to rely on is the teachings of AA members the effect is quite different. All that the inductees know is that they're being asked to be humble and, as with all of the other word games that AA plays, that is enough to keep the member coming back so AA can continue their indoctrination. That's why I wrote this book; so people would be able to understand *exactly* what AA is telling them and so they can make an informed choice as to whether the religion of Alcoholics Anonymous is something that they actually want. To this end, I believe that a little bit of word substitution might shine some light on this word-play of AA's.

I have described many of AA's instances of double talk. If you take a close look at all of these semantic games that AA utilizes in this Step, you can deduce just how steeped in religion this Step is. Up to this point, they have been building up phrases that they use to disguise AA's religion as medicine. They start using these heavily in this Step, and it provides AA a way of posing as a fellowship rather than the highly dogmatic church that it is. Let's start our word substitution with the star of this chapter, 'humility'. When I replace 'humility' with what AA admits is their definition of 'humility', it brings into stark relief how religious their program is and how their policy of using everyday language in place of their theology works to hide AA's true goal; indoctrination.

"Indeed, the ~~attainment of greater humility~~ desire

to seek and do God's will is the foundation of each... step"

"Our crippling handicap had been our lack of ~~humility~~ desire to seek and do God's will"

"so it is that we first see ~~humility~~ a desire to seek and do God's will as a necessity"

"the whole emphasis of Step Seven is on ~~humility~~ our desire to seek and do God's will"

Now let's look at the text of the Step itself, the part about 'shortcomings'. While AA has used this word earlier in the program, as is there wont they kept the meaning of that word unclear lest the member should connect the dots and get close to the truth sooner than AA would wish. In this Step they clarify that by 'shortcomings' they mean the character defects that they spoke of in Step Four. *"But when we had taken a square look at some of these defects... and have become willing to have them removed"*. It's worth noting that they just kind of slip that in- AA gives no warning or reason. They simply talk of having the "defects" removed and then subtly change it to "have our shortcomings removed" and that then becomes the text of this Step. Looking back, it at Step Four that AA defined these character defects as the Seven Deadly Sins of

Christian teachings.

This is simply a continuation of that strategy of giving dual meanings to words, and phrases, thus allowing them deniability when their program is called a religion. In this way, while hiding the definitions of those words, they can defend themselves by saying that ridding ourselves of shortcomings is a noble pursuit for anyone. What they hide, however, is that shortcomings = character defects = the Seven Deadly Sins of the Christian religion. Getting back to the bright light of word substitution, we can tell what AA is actually telling us in this Step;

"Still goaded by sheer necessity, we reluctantly come to grips with those ~~serious character flaws~~ Seven Deadly Sins that made problem drinkers of us in the first place"

"We will want to be rid of some of these ~~defects~~ Seven Deadly Sins..."

"But when we had taken a square look at some of these ~~defects~~ Seven Deadly Sins ... and have become willing to have them removed"

In the last paragraph of the 12x12 Book's chapter on Step, Seven, the obfuscation of AA's true meanings of the words is at its most intense, bringing many of their deceits together in that one paragraph; *"The Seventh Step is where we make the change in our attitude which permits us, with ~~humility~~ (the desire to seek and do God's will) as our guide, to move out from ourselves toward others and towards God. The whole emphasis is on ~~humility~~ (the desire to seek and do God's will). It is really saying that we now ought to be willing to try ~~humility~~ (to have a desire to seek and do God's will) in seeking the removal of our ~~shortcomings~~ (Seven Deadly Sins) just as we did when we admitted that we were powerless over alcohol, and came to believe that a ~~Power~~ g0~~reater~~ ~~than~~ ~~ourselves~~ (a God we love and call by name) could restore us to sanity".*

If this is how someone want to live their life, great. But they have a right make an informed decision.

STEPS Eight & Nine- Eh!

<u>Steps Eight & Nine: Made a list of all persons we had harmed, and became willing to make amends to them all and made direct amends to such people wherever possible, except when to do so would injure them or others</u>.

Steps Eight & Nine are the only two Steps in the entire program that are not particularly religious. The mandated confession to God for our Sins has already taken place and the whole idea in these two Steps seems to be to de-clutter one's mind and conscience where it relates to human beings. AA seems to believe that once we have acknowledged, and atoned for, whatever wrongs we have committed that the exercise of sobriety will be a smoother path. Whether that is true or not is certainly open to debate, but it is also beyond the scope of this book which is only aimed at explaining the deeply religious nature of the Twelve Steps. With Step Ten, however, AA resumes its indoctrination and its use of dual definitions.

STEP Ten- Lots of Sin, Lots of Praying

<u>Step Ten: Continued to take personal inventory and when we were wrong promptly admitted it.</u>

In this Step, AA directs us to increase our prayer periods to several times daily, with annual and semi-annual major rituals along with multi-day prayer "retreats".

When AA inductees first enter the program, they are all told that AA is not a religious program. As this book has painstakingly detailed, the program is actually a fundamentalist faith-healing sect of Christianity. In this Step, and through the rest of the Steps, AA begins using deeply religious terms as an exclamation mark at the end of their program while forsaking some of the deep camouflage so prevalent earlier in the program. While Alcoholics Anonymous will NEVER admit they lied, their words in these final three Steps show little more than passing concern with hiding the religiosity of their program. After all, at this point they have had enormous time to convert their members to their religion and, at this point, either it worked or it didn't.

Step Ten begins a three-step process of jettisoning any religious beliefs that are not in lock-step with the Alcoholics Anonymous religion. After taking a break in Steps Eight and Nine, AA begins an upwards trajectory in religious fervor which concludes with a "spiritual awakening" which will *"open the channel so that where there had been a trickle, there now was a river which led to sure power and safe guidance from God as we were increasingly better able to understand Him"*. Having gone from promising us that our own conception of God would suffice, AA now shows us that they meant 'until we can make you understand Him differently- as AA understands Him'.

AA starts off its 12x12 Book chapter on Step Ten by speaking of 'liabilities' in its second paragraph. As we saw in Step Four, when Alcoholics Anonymous refers to 'liabilities' they are using everyday words to talk about the Seven Deadly Sins of Christianity. In keeping with AA's stated policy of disguising their theology with everyday words, they use the wording of this Step to apply a secular mask to an extremely religious exercise. While instructing its member to take a "personal inventory" they are actually directing their membership to look within themselves for how they have committed Deadly Sin. This simply continues their core philosophy that was shown earlier; the cause of alcoholism is sinning and the cure is to have God personally lift the obsession to drink out of alcoholics.

Step Ten is actually a continuation of Steps Six and Seven. In those Steps AA had its members look at how they had committed the Seven Deadly

Sins and then asked God to remove that Sin from their souls. In this Step, AA wants that that soul-searching-for-sin to be turned into an every-day (and more) activity. AA declares that "*a continuous look at our assets and liabilities...are necessities...no one can make much of his life until self-searching becomes a regular habit*".

AA recommends that this 'self-searching' for the Seven Deadly Sins be taken several times every day. They list a spot-check, taken at various times during the day; one at the end of every day; another kind that they refer to as 'semi-annual housecleanings and, to cap things off, an occasional retreat from the outside world for a solid day or two. The purpose of all of these 'checks' is made clear in AA's description of the spot-check; "Not my will, but Thine, be done".

While no particularly new religious exercises come out of this Step, this is where AA convinces its members to engage in prayer and worship several times a day, every day as well as to set long periods aside each year to do nothing but worship. For this is AA's answer to alcoholism; intense prayer to a God you will love and call by name.

STEP Eleven- AA and the God of The Atom

Step Eleven: Sought through prayer and meditation to improve our conscious contact with God as we understood Him, praying only for knowledge of His will for us and the power to carry that out.

Step11 is where AA abandons all claims of secularism and jumps into the deep end of the Christianity pool with the enthusiasm and abandon of a little boy in a rain puddle. Here is where AA has finally driven the disbelief from us and where we finally surrender our will to AA's God. In this Step, AA shows us how we finally saw the light of their God's glory, and where we finally accepted that atheism and agnosticism are simply states of denial.

The very first sentence in the 12x12 chapter on Step Eleven clearly indicates that AA, has dropped its subterfuge (though AA still tries to confuse potential members by using the religious 'prayer' and the more secular 'meditation' interchangeably) and will now commence to full-throatedly advocate for God, Prayer and Salvation; *"Prayer and meditation are our principal means of conscious contact with God"*. The first two pages of this chapter are dedicated to detailing how atheists and agnostics came to realize how wrong they were and *"were sold on meditation and prayer"*. The fervor that AA pours into this chapter is disturbing; its zealotry and frenzy seem pre-orgasmic and with good reason; the program is approaching its climax in the next Step, AA's final Step Twelve. That will mark the member's completed conversion and they will have their marching orders to proselytize for the Alcoholics Anonymous religion.

Step Eleven is, from beginning to end, an exultation of the miracle that AA has been leading up to with their entire program. Completely absent is any pretense about AA not being a religion. In its place is a detailed account of how the atheist, having been nursed through the program with various crutches, finally accepts God onto his heart and rejoices at finding that he had been wrong his entire life; that there was indeed a God and, as soon as the atheist retired from the 'debating society', he was able to find "...*God with His grace, wisdom, and love*". This Step is so utterly swamped in religious fervor, that it could be used as an early warning system for those who don't seek religious indoctrination; the 12x12 instructions for this Step serve as a review of the lies that AA has told.

When we entered the program we were told that all we had to do was admit we were powerless over alcohol and agree to accept the AA group as a Higher Power in order to make our lives, once again, manageable. What AA didn't reveal is that "group as a Higher Power" is simply a tool to

connect the agnostics and atheists with what AA
believes are non-believers' true beliefs about God.
AA teaches that atheists and agnostics, because they
actually possess an innate belief in God, are simply
in denial. Step Eleven tells us; *"To certain
newcomers and to those one-time agnostics..."*
(notice the "one-time") *"...who still cling to the AA
group as their higher power, claims for the power
of prayer may...still be unconvincing...We well
remember how something deep inside us kept
rebelling against the idea of bowing before any
God".* According to Step Eleven agnostics believed
that *"No doubt the universe had a first cause of
some sort, the God of the Atom, maybe... But
certainly there wasn't any evidence of a God who
knew or cared about human beings..."* But then we
finally saw the light of AA's God; *"We liked AA all
right, and were quick to say that it had done
miracles.... Of course, we finally did experiment,
and when unexpected results followed, we felt
different; in fact we knew different; and so we were
sold on meditation and prayer. And that, we have
found, can happen to anybody who tries".* AA's
true attitude towards non-believers is made crystal
clear in this Step, should you have needed any
clarification; there are no non-believers, just
Christians who have not yet seen the light.

To Alcoholics Anonymous, *everyone*
believes in God; those people who claim to be

atheists and agnostics are in denial and just need AA to straighten them out, willing or not. Agnostics, we see, actually believe in both miracles and the Christian tale of Creation (though for agnostics, it's called *'first cause'* by the *'God of the Atom')*. Structured around this conceit, Alcoholics Anonymous dictates that all atheists and agnostics should have no trouble working the AA program as long as they're *willing* to change from who they are into people who pray several times a day to a God who will heal disease when AA tells Him to, as long as they're *willing* to pray to a God that will magically *lift* disease out of AA adherents and as long as they're *willing* to become good Christians; after all, "*deep down in every man, woman, and child, is the fundamental idea of God*". That is how Alcoholics Anonymous is able to justify their lies and deceit; to AA, there is only one religion- theirs- and all people believe in it whether they know it or not. Since AA believes that *all* people have an innate belief in AA's God, Alcoholics Anonymous feels justified in tricking people because they're only showing them the TRUTH; if you disagree, that's just your disease talking. Once members accept this theological house of mirrors, Step Eleven then links this acceptance of God to the previous Steps dealing with their 'moral inventory' - the search for the Seven Deadly Sins of Christian theology.

Step Eleven reinforces AA's core philosophy- that the Seven Deadly Sins are the root cause of alcoholism- by explicitly linking prayer, the search for Sin (the 'moral inventory'), and Heaven; *"There is a direct linkage among self-examination, meditation and prayer... when they are logically related and interwoven... we may be granted a glimpse of that ultimate reality which is God's kingdom And... our own destiny in that realm will be secure so long as we... do the will of our own Creator".* Where in the beginning Alcoholics Anonymous assured us that religion would not be required, Step Eleven now dictates that such thoughts have no place in AA.

Not only does Step Eleven require prayer to a living God but it goes as far as giving instruction in how to pray, giving us the text of a Christian prayer to recite and telling us that we are not allowed to refuse these instructions. Lecturing on prayer, AA claims that *"The actual experience of meditation and prayer across the centuries is... immense... It is hoped that every AA who has a religious connection which emphasizes meditation will return to the practice of that devotion... But... the rest of us... might start like this. First, let's look at a really good prayer... Its author... has been rated as a saint..."* The prayer begins thusly; *"Lord, make me a channel of thy peace...",* rambles on in prayer to the 'Lord', and ends with *"It is by dying that one wakens the Eternal Life. Amen"*. AA, that bastion of non-religious healing, advises *"...we might reread that prayer several times very slowly, savoring every word and trying to take in the deep meaning..."* after which AA explicitly bars any argument with this religious instruction and instructs members to abandon all agnosticism or atheism; *"It will help if we can drop all resistance to what our friend says. For in meditation, debate has no place"*. Alcoholics Anonymous is clear on this point; *shut up and do as you're told!"* Though that message is pretty clear, they still like to play games. One they play here is the constant intermingling of the words 'prayer' and 'meditation'.

When dealing with most people, the use of multiple words for the same idea is common and harmless. With Alcoholics Anonymous, however, caution is merited due to the fact that their whole indoctrination is based on wordplay, substitution and concealment. Of most immediate note would be their deliberate confusion of the words 'spiritual' and 'religious'; with the cynical conflating of those two terms, Alcoholics Anonymous has deliberately provided cover for about 95% of substance abuse treatment centers and innumerable governmental bodies to force millions of citizens into the Church of Alcoholics Anonymous. These entities may be barred from forcing people into religion, but they feel comfortable forcing people into 'spiritual' programs. Though there is no real difference between the two, the use of synonyms seems to make it OK. AA is simply using the same trickery when they conflate the words 'meditation' and 'prayer'.

While the words 'prayer' and 'meditation' usually have significant difference, when Alcoholics Anonymous uses them they are synonymous, as we saw above when they referred to meditation as *"the practice of ... devotion"*. Just to be clear, the meaning of devotion is

> a: religious fervor : PIETY
>
> b: an act of prayer or private worship — usually used in plural
>
> c: a religious exercise or practice other than the regular corporate worship of a congregation

Don't be fooled; when Alcoholics Anonymous directs members to meditate, they are instructing them to pray. The wording of Step Eleven has a specific purpose; when a prospect first approaches AA, they are presented with the Twelve Steps. If AA said what they actually mean, anyone who didn't want to join a faith-healing sect of Christianity would never come back. AA had to find ways to fool people into disbelieving their own common sense, so they came up with phrases like "God as you understand Him", "Spiritual not

Religious", "AA group as your Higher Power", etc. Using the word 'meditation' in the place of the word 'prayer' is simply more of that same tactic of plausible deniability; AA can protest that meditation is secular with one side of their mouths while out the other side they define meditation as 'devotion', a religious fervor. That is the last bait-and-switch before AA closes the deal and directs the member to have what they euphemistically call a 'spiritual awakening'.

This 'Spiritual Awakening' perhaps best reflects how the founders of Alcoholics Anonymous were so influenced by the Oxford Groups (a Christian organization that was very popular at the time of AA's founding) as well as the main difference between them and AA. Without getting too much into the Oxford Groups- it's a bit outside of the scope of this book- the relationship between them is important in understanding why the 'Spiritual Awakening' is the last Step of the program. Alcoholics Anonymous is based heavily on the teachings and de-centralized structure of the Oxford Group, as it was originally a part of the Oxford Group before Bob and Bill split off from them. A major difference between the two is the timing of the 'Spiritual Awakening'; in the Oxford Group, inductees had to 'witness'- swear in front of the group their belief in Christianity- *before* being granted membership. AA saw that as a problem in recruitment and understood that it would hinder their ambition to use alcoholism as a means to indoctrinate as many non-believers as possible into Christianity. It also didn't help AA's public relations strategy that the founder of the Oxford Groups, Dr. Frank Buchman, was a cheerleader for Adolf Hitler and the Nazis. In order to fulfill their ambitions of Christian indoctrination, AA split off from the Oxford Groups and constructed a program designed to mask its intense religiosity with "*everyday language*" and indoctrinate unwitting victims into Christian theology until they have a 'Spiritual Awakening'.

The two main texts of Alcoholics Anonymous, the 'Big Book' and 'Twelve Steps and Twelve Traditions' serve only one purpose; indoctrination of people under the guise of medicine. Once Alcoholics Anonymous convinced the member that praying to God for the knowledge of His will wasn't religious, and was the key to curing alcoholism, they then commenced on a campaign to show us that the Seven Deadly Sins are the cause of all alcoholism and have nothing to do with religion. While trying to convince members that they are not practicing religion, AA sent them on a quest to root out the Seven Deadly Sins of Christian theology within themselves. This quest for Sin is at the center of the program, both spiritually and logistically. Logistically speaking, the Steps that came before were designed to prepare the member for that quest and the Steps that are still to come serve the purpose of atoning, and asking forgiveness, for those Sins. Spiritually, the Seven Deadly Sins are the cause of alcoholism.

The path to AA's 'Spiritual Awakening' has been one filled with lies and misdirection. Without a guide to lead one through the thickets of religious fervor, a normal person would find themselves bogged down in ancient Christian theology and rituals before they even realized that they were being converted. Step Twelve marks the conclusion of that convoluted journey from normalcy to religious fervor.

STEP Twelve- Born Again, Whether You Want It Or Not

Step Twelve: Having had a spiritual awakening as a result of these steps, we tried to carry this message to alcoholics, and to practice these principles in all our affairs.

Step Twelve involves two distinct events; we conclude the process which could best be described as AA's version of being Born Again and we commence to proselytize for the religion of Alcoholics Anonymous.

In this chapter of AA's 12x12 Book, AA reveals that the point of the Twelve Steps is to have a Spiritual Awakening. AA likes to be as opaque as possible when discussing the religion that is their program, so they use this "Spiritual Awakening" phrase so they can employ their defense of "spiritual not religious". This Spiritual Awakening, however, is described in the Big Book chapter "We Agnostics".

Examining that chapter, we can see Alcoholics Anonymous' peculiar approach to this type of personal religious upheaval. While there are many religions who want you to get saved, or born again, or in some form 'see the light', AA is the only religion to claim that we all believe in God when we are born; "*deep down in every man, woman, and child, is the fundamental idea of God... faith in some kind of God was a part of our makeup"*. This arrogance is at the root of their claims that anyone can work their program; since *everyone* believes in God, *everyone* can commit their lives to seeking the knowledge of His will and to rooting out how they have sinned against Him. Atheists and agnostics can work the program because, after all, *"...we were fooling ourselves..."* This arrogance is illustrated when they describe this "spiritual awakening".

In the 12x12 Book, AA discusses this Spiritual Awakening by reviewing the previous eleven Steps, employing their usual technique of obscuring their religion by using the code words that they have developed over the course of the Steps. In order to understand what has truly occurred, as opposed to what AA is *telling* us has occurred, those code words will need to be translated. Of course, this is just more of the same thing that we have seen over the course of the AA program. In starting this discussion, AA asks *"What do you mean when you talk about a spiritual awakening?... In a very real sense he has been transformed... What he has received is a free gift, and yet usually, at least in some small part, he has made himself ready to receive it. AA's manner of making ready to receive this gift lies in the practice of the Twelve Steps"*. AA then commences to review the Steps already taken.

AA tells us that in Step One *"We... first*

admitted that we were powerless over..." alcohol. What AA leaves out is that a 'necessity' of this admission was a "desire to seek and do God's will". AA then proceeds to Step Two to assert that "*since we could not restore ourselves to sanity, some Higher Power must necessarily do so...*" but leaves out that that Higher Power has a specific identity; he "*who still considered his well-loved AA group the higher power would presently love God and call Him by name*". Proceeding to Step Three, AA tells us that in order to 'turn our will and lives over to God' we could use the AA group as that God. What they hide is that after we worked this Step, AA turned around and told us that what we actually did was turned our "*will and life over to a newfound Providence*", which is defined as 'divine guidance' and 'God conceived as the power sustaining and guiding human destiny'. Reviewing Step Four, AA describes the Step as a search for "*the things in ourselves which had brought us to physical, moral and spiritual bankruptcy*". What they don't reveal is that they are actually referring to the Seven Deadly Sins of ancient Christian theology. Alcoholics Anonymous continues this cherry-picking review of their Steps, employing their standard public relation campaign of selling faith-healing as secular medicine through the rest of their program. When this review gets to Step Eleven, they begin the discussion of the 'spiritual awakening'.

It is here that AA jettisons the idea that non-believers have a place in Alcoholics Anonymous other than as targets of religious indoctrination. Also of help in understanding the intensely religious nature of the entire program is the description of a spiritual awakening in the Big Books chapter 'We Agnostics'. In the 12x12 book, a somewhat generic description of this religious upheaval is related; *"The persistent use of meditation and prayer, we found, did open the channel so that where there had been a trickle, there now was a river which led to sure power and safe guidance from God as we were increasingly better able to understand Him. So, practicing these Steps, we had a spiritual awakening about which finally there was no question... we could predict that the doubter... who still considered his well-loved AA group the higher power, would presently love God and call Him by name"*. Of course, AA will always protest that their program is not religious. If you've read this book this far and still believe that, I'm not sure what could ever convince you. But the description of the spiritual awakening in the Big Book's chapter 'We Agnostics' is as good of a place to turn to as any.

In this chapter of the Big Book, AA relates the story of *"...a man who thought he was an atheist"*. 'Thought he was'- again, to AA, everyone is born with a belief in God. *"One night, he was approached by an alcoholic who had known a spiritual experience. Our friends gorge rose as he bitterly cried out: 'If there is a God, He certainly hasn't done anything for me'.... Then, like a thunderbolt, a great thought came. It crowded out all else. 'Who are you to say there is no God?' This man recounts that he tumbled out of bed to his knees. In a few seconds he was overwhelmed by a conviction of the Presence of God. It poured over and through him... He stood in the Presence of Infinite Power and Love. He had stepped from bridge to shore. For the first time, he lived in conscious companionship with his Creator".* This is what Alcoholics Anonymous sells to the world as "not religious", and they give explicit instructions to their members to swear that their program is secular while they fulfill the other half of Step Twelve; proselytizing.

Just as with so many religions, AA commands their followers to spread their gospel but, unlike other religions, AA instructs its followers to hide the religious nature of AA from those they preach to. AA has been so successful with this strategy that governments- and almost the entire substance abuse treatment industry- have been able to order millions of United States citizens into the AA religion, using this lie by Alcoholics Anonymous to sidestep the First Amendment and patients' rights laws and policies that normally protect against such forced indoctrination. From AA's beginning days, they have given explicit instructions to their members to conceal the program's religious nature.

In the Big Book chapter 'Working With Others' and in the 12x12 Book, AA explicitly tells their members to hide AA's religiosity when recruiting non-believers into Alcoholics Anonymous. Labeling non-believers as 'belligerent savages', AA denounces those non-believers' beliefs as "prejudiced" and "confused" and instructs their recruiters to *"use everyday language to describe spiritual principles. There is no use arousing any prejudice he may have against certain theological terms and conceptions about which he may already be confused. Don't raise such issues... Let him see that you are not there to instruct him in religion"*. We can see this policy in play in the public relations of AA when they declare to the world that they are "spiritual, not religious".

Step twelve concludes the program of alcoholics anonymous by having their members undergo a religious upheaval after which they sally forth into the world to indoctrinate others as they have been indoctrinated.

CHAPTER 3
The Real Alcoholics Anonymous

In this chapter, I have written the Alcoholics Anonymous method of recovery while stripping away all of the prevarication and duplicity that AA buries their theology in. By necessity, it will be far shorter than AA's explanation of its program because all of the untruths have been removed. I'm putting this chapter in for a very good reason; I believe in freedom of conscience and self-determination.

Reading this book, it would be a mistake to attribute anti-religion hostility to me. I couldn't care less whether someone wants to pray or not. In a way, I even support it; if the love you need can be found by believing that there is an entity in the sky who loves and cares for you, who am I to spite you that warmth? If that love is what propels you to decency and kindness, who am I to sneer at that? If you're an alcoholic and you need religion to stop drinking, I say 'more power to you and good luck'. If believing in miracles is the key to happiness for you, have at it. No, it's not AA's religion that I have a problem with; it's the trickery, lies and the deliberate efforts to have people forced into their program that I find incredibly problematic and dangerous (though AA would argue that they are not involved in force- I will get to that). The fact that it will always be people in a state of distress that comes to AA compounds the problem; AA becomes predatory.

People come to AA under pretty much three conditions; their minds are compromised by alcohol, they are there under orders of either the courts or a rehab, or both. If a person is there with no coercion of any kind, in all likelihood their minds are impaired by alcohol abuse. Because AA has been accepted and promoted by the substance abuse treatment as legitimate treatment, AA carries with it a stamp of legitimacy. AA exploits that cloak of legitimacy by exploiting the impaired minds of potential inductees; instead of being upfront and telling the potential member that they are to embark on a religious trek in which they seek a miracle from the Christian 'Creator', they lie and tell them that Alcoholics Anonymous "is not a religious society". The reason has, of course, been explained in the earlier chapters of this book but it bears repeating; they lie in order to indoctrinate their targets into their fundamentalist, faith-healing sect of Christianity. That these targets are suffering from alcohol abuse becomes a tool for AA; they bury their theology in word games to confuse the members into believing that they are wrong when they interpret AA doctrine for the theology that it is and berate them as belligerent savages should they continue to balk. Should Alcoholics Anonymous never be able to overcome the intelligence of the inductee, and never convince him that the religion of Alcoholics Anonymous is not religious, they still win. A key part of Step Twelve, just as with any other religion, is proselytizing. By lying about its religious nature, AA members are able to exploit the resistant member for much longer than if they told the truth upfront. When the member smartens up and stops attending AA's meetings, the amount of time Alcoholics Anonymous was able to con him into staying is that much more time that its members have had to stroke their own egos and that many more pew seats that AA has filled. AA has no qualms about how they fill their pews, and force is just another tool for them. When they lie people into their meetings, it's pretty low but when they use *force* to fill their pews they become despicable and dangerous.

I myself was forced to attend AA, with Alcoholics Anonymous playing an active and key role in that force. AA will stridently argue that they have no part in forcing people into their meetings, but AA voluntarily fills a role that is indispensable to that compulsory attendance; they sign attendance sheets which are the monitoring tool used to confirm attendance.

When attendance is required at AA meetings by either a government agency or a rehabilitation clinic, the person being forced to attend is provided with attendance sheets that must be signed by the AA group. After sitting through a meeting, all of the forced attendees line up to have these sheets signed by a ranking member of whatever AA group's meeting they're attending. This sheet is then submitted back to the government, or treatment team, as proof of attendance. The immediate effect of this tacit agreement between government (or treatment professionals) and Alcoholics Anonymous is that AA reports attendance at their religious meetings to the government. Alcoholics Anonymous always argues against this point by claiming that they are just doing what the attendees ask, but the clear knowledge on AA's part of the compulsory nature of these sheets renders that protest as disingenuous at best. When we look at how much power the courts and rehabilitation clinics have to threaten people into submission to the religion of Alcoholics Anonymous, this attendance monitoring becomes frightening.

My personal experience with these threats can best illustrate how Alcoholics Anonymous can threaten peoples' freedom. When I was convicted of DWI I was sentenced to three years' probation, with attendance at AA mandated as well as participation in an alcohol treatment program. My problems started immediately, as I protested the religious content of AA to both my probation officer and the treatment staff at the treatment program I attended. The hostility and threats I received were remarkable. My probation officer increased both the amounts and types of AA programs I was required to attend, ordering me to go to specialized meetings such as ones that were sort of like workshops, but the staff at my outpatient program were particularly vicious. Unless I agreed to honor, support and agree with AA doctrine, I was informed that they would direct me to be committed to a locked mental health facility- an insane asylum- until I was converted. Because AA has so intertwined itself in our institutions, I was forced to attest allegiance to Alcoholics Anonymous religion in order to prevent commitment to an insane asylum. THAT is how dangerous Alcoholics Anonymous is to a free people- submit to AA religion or be committed.

For those of you who are just being introduced to AA, I hope this translation of Alcoholics Anonymous doctrine will help prevent your unwilling indoctrination.

The Twelve Steps of Alcoholics Anonymous
What Alcoholics Anonymous Actually Means

1. We admitted we were powerless over alcohol that our lives had become unmanageable without God.

2. Came to believe God would lift my alcoholism from me with a miracle.

3. Made a decision to turn our will and our lives over to the care of the God of the Bible that I will learn to love and call by name.

4. Made a searching and fearless inventory for how we have committed the Seven Deadly Sins.

5. Admitted to God, to ourselves, and to another human how we have committed Sin.

6. Were entirely ready to have God remove all these Seven Deadly Sins from our souls.

7. Humbly asked Him to remove all of these Seven Deadly Sins from our souls.

8. Made a list of all persons we had harmed, and became willing to make amends to them all.

9. Made direct amends to such people wherever possible, except when to do so would injure them or others.

10. Continued to take personal inventory of how we have committed the Seven Deadly Sins and when we sinned promptly admitted it.

11. Sought through prayer and meditation to improve our conscious contact with the Christian God that we love and call by name, praying only for

knowledge of His will for us and the power to carry that out.

12. Having had a spiritual awakening to a God-consciousness as a result of these steps, we tried to lure other alcoholics into the AA religion whether they wanted our religion or not, and to practice these rituals in all our affairs.

Step One: We admitted we were powerless over alcohol that our lives had become unmanageable without God.

We admit complete defeat and agree that we can accomplish nothing without God. The reason for this is that, though alcoholism is recognized as a disease, the only cure is to have God lift that alcoholism out of us with a miracle. When we seek this miracle, self-sufficiency and self-confidence are our enemies; we must commit to do ONLY as God commands because alcoholism is NEVER cured except through a miracle. In the ensuing Steps, we will learn how to get closer to God so that he may bestow his miracle upon us. We must have no doubt; being Alcoholics Anonymous, we know the mind of God and when we ask he WILL grant our request.

But what if our life is still manageable? We still must admit complete defeat and agree to become a believer in faith-healing Christianity because of other AAers experience. If we don't immediately engage in faith-healing, we will die.

Step Two: Came to believe God would lift our alcoholism from us with a miracle.

We commit to seek and do God's will. This is a necessity to work the program because we are pursuing a miracle.

Step Three: Made a decision to turn our will and our lives over to the care of the God of the Bible that I will learn to love and call by name.

We conclude that we are incapable of living without God and, seeking God to bestow a miracle on us, we agree to do His will and His will only. If we are atheist or agnostic, we realize that we are belligerent savages and commit to abandon those beliefs and commit our lives to prayer to the Creator.

Step Four: Made a searching and fearless inventory for how we have committed the Seven Deadly Sins.

We searched our souls to find where we have committed the Seven Deadly Sins, recognizing that Sin is the sole and only cause of alcoholism.

Step Five: Admitted to God, to ourselves, and to another human how we have committed Sin.

We confessed our sins to God. We also confessed to other people so we knew that our

God's guidance was acceptable to AA.

Step Six: Were entirely ready to have God remove all these Seven Deadly Sins from our souls.

We prayed to God, preparing to ask Him to remove the Sin from our souls.

Step Seven: Humbly asked Him to remove our remove all these Seven Deadly Sins from our souls.

We prayed to God, asking Him to remove the Sin from our souls.

Step Eight: Made a list of all persons we had harmed, and became willing to make amends to them all.

No translation needed, for the most part

Step Nine: Made direct amends to such people wherever possible, except when to do so would injure them or others.

No translation needed, for the most part

Step Ten: Continued to take personal inventory of how we have committed the Seven Deadly Sins and when we sinned promptly admitted it.

We continued to search our souls for the Seven Deadly Sins.

Step Eleven: Sought through prayer and meditation

to improve our conscious contact with the Christian God that we love and call by name, praying only for knowledge of His will for us and the power to carry that out.

We commenced to praying several times a day to our Creator, and to take day-long, or multi-day long, batches of time from our lives to do nothing but pray to that Creator. We abandoned any beliefs out of line with the religion of Alcoholics Anonymous and lived our life ONLY according to AA theology.

Step Twelve: Having been born again as a result of these steps, we tried to lure other alcoholics into the AA religion whether they wanted our religion or not, and to practice the AA religion in all our affairs.

We were born again and committed our lives to proselytizing.

CHAPTER 4
A Self Defense Primer

The reason that I wrote this book is to help people protect themselves from involuntary, and unwitting, indoctrination. I hope that I have provided a clear explanation of the methods and tools that Alcoholics Anonymous uses to convert people to its religion. I hope that once the reader has read into the book this far they will have a strong grasp of the tricks that AA will play on them and, so, won't fall for them. Though I believe I have explained that trickery fairly well, I believe that the intricate, winding, twisted and involved nature of their indoctrination makes defense against their mind games difficult even if you have read this entire book.

AA's members have had decades to hone their responses, and to challenge their pat responses on the fly can be difficult. If an AA member answers "It's only God *as we understand Him*" when challenged on AA's core philosophy of healing through God's miracle, it's difficult to wade through AA literature, and this book, to retort that AA really means "*a God we love and call by name*" and "*the Creator*". Because AA members go to hours of AA meetings every week, and even multi-day AA retreats, they receive endless hours of training on how to camouflage their faith-healing theology in everyday terms and, thus, AA members are well practiced at their dishonest debate techniques while everyone else is at a disadvantage in calling them on their lies. That is where I hope this chapter will come in handy.

In this chapter, you will find a short synopsis of each Step's manipulations and obfuscations with references to what AA is hiding and how they're trying to trick you. I would recommend making a photo copy of this chapter for quick reference (you have my expressed permission to make one copy of this section of this book for your own personal use) so when you're at an AA meeting you will be able to quickly understand what you are being told. If you like what Alcoholics Anonymous is actually trying to get you to do- great! I wish you the best of luck in your journey. If you *don't* like what Alcoholics Anonymous is actually trying to get you to do, at least you will be able to navigate your way through AA's maze of untruths with a clear map.

Step One: We admitted we were powerless over alcohol that our lives had become unmanageable.

The first thing Alcoholics Anonymous tells you as a new member is that they are not religious, but the truth is that AA declares that an act of God is the only thing that can cure alcoholism. "*...only* *an act of Providence can remove it... (Step 1)"* and that *"No... human willpower could break it (Step 1)"*.

This Step prepares you to accept a Higher Power. Here, they claim that that 'Higher Power' can be the AA group, but they later reveal that they really mean A God that we *"would presently love... and call Him by name" (Step 12)*.

AA claims to only offer 'suggestions' but in reality issues religious ultimatums; *"Until he so humbles himself, his sobriety- if any- will be precarious"(Step 1)*. They hide from the member what they actually mean by 'humble'; *"a desire to seek and do God's will" (Step 7)*.

Step One requires the belief in a God that we will love and call by name.

Step Two: Came to believe that A Power Greater than Ourselves could restore us to sanity.

AA says publicly that their 'Power Greater than Ourselves' can be anything that the member chooses, but this is nothing more than subterfuge; he *"who still considered his well-loved AA the group the higher power, would presently love God and call Him by name" (Step 12)*.

Alcoholics Anonymous uses that subterfuge to falsely claim that non-believers can work the AA program, but makes clear their feelings towards those non-believers; *"Let's look at the case of the one who says he won't believe- the belligerent one. He is in a state of mind which can be described only as savage" (Step 2)*

Non-believers are only welcome in Alcoholics Anonymous as a target of religious conversion. AA explicitly, savagely condemns their beliefs.

Step Three: Made a decision to turn our will and our lives over to the care of God as we understood Him,

Here, we find the big public relations stunt of Alcoholics Anonymous, pretending that God can be anything we choose. However, AA has made it clear that a specific understanding of God is fundamental, and absolutely indispensable, to Alcoholics Anonymous; the entire program is based on the belief that AA's God performs miracles and lift disease out of AA members, "...*only an act of Providence can remove it...(Step 1)*" and that "*No... human willpower could break it (Step 1)*", "*when I ... then asked... God as I understand Him... my obsession to drink vanished. It was lifted right out of me*" *(Step 6).*

The God of Alcoholics Anonymous is not a flexible belief; AA's God is a living God who will intervene in human affairs and, when AA members ask, will heal disease.

Step Four: Made a searching and fearless moral

<u>inventory of ourselves.</u>

Alcoholics Anonymous denies that religion and faith-healing are an integral, and inseparable, part of AA but this Step clearly contradicts this premise. This Step, so important to AA, requires each AA member to take part in Christian worship; this is a search for how we have committed the Seven Deadly Sins Of ancient Christian teachings. The entire program of Alcoholics Anonymous revolves around this Christianity because AA dictates that those Sins are the sole cause of Alcoholism

AA religion incorporates the Christian biblical story of Creation by a living God and dictates that instincts were bestowed on us by that God during Creation; *"Creation gave us instincts for a purpose. So these desires... are perfectly necessary and right, and surely God-given..."* However, *"these instincts... often exceed their proper functions.. When that happens... the instincts... have turned to liabilities"*. AA reveals that its entire program is based on ancient Christian teachings about Sin, that it is those Sins that cause alcoholism and it is those Sins that are the target of the 'moral inventory'; *"Alcoholics should be able to see that instinct run wild in themselves is the underlying cause of their destructive drinking... To avoid falling into confusion over the names these defects should be called, let's take a universally recognized list of major human failings- the Seven Deadly Sins of pride, greed, lust, anger, gluttony, envy, and sloth" (All references can be found in Step 4).*

AA believes that Sinning against God causes alcoholism and after you have confessed your sins through the AA method, God will magically heal your disease.

Step Five: Admitted to God, to ourselves, and to another human being the exact nature of our wrongs.

AA denies that they practice religion, but this Step expressly requires the confession of the Seven Deadly Sins; *"...relief never came by confessing the sins of other people. Everybody has to confess their own" (Step 5)* (Note; if you raise this point to an AA member and they deny that they are referring to the biblical Seven Deadly Sins, point them back to the references previously cited for Step Four's 'moral inventory').

AA further points out that our own understanding of God actually doesn't suffice, putting lie to their earlier Steps. While explaining why we have to confess to another person in addition to God, AA explains; *"what comes to us alone may be garbled by our own rationalization and wishful thinking... How many times have we heard well-intentioned people claim the guidance of*

107

God when it was all too plain that they were sorely mistaken?" AA does not allow someone to understand God's message to them without AA approval of that message.

Alcoholics Anonymous demands that members seek out how they have violated the Christian God's Seven Deadly Sins and requires AA approval for the members understanding of God.

Step Six: Were entirely ready to have God remove all these defects of character.

AA promotes their program as 'not religious' but, rather, secular medicine. In reality their program is faith-healing, with AA declaring that they know the mind of God; *"the... question of whether God can- and will, under certain circumstances- remove defects of character will be answered with a prompt affirmative by almost any AA member ...this... is no theory... it will be just about the largest fact in his life... when I asked ... God, as I understood Him, to give me release, my obsession to drink vanished"* *"It is plain for everybody to see that each sober AA member has been granted a release from this... fatal obsession".*

AA claims that 'God' is only meant 'as we understood Him', but AA makes it clear that they mean 'God' and His miracle of healing literally- not figuratively, but literally; *"So in a very complete and literal way, all AAs have become entirely ready to have God remove the mania for alcohol from their lives. And God has proceeded to do exactly that".*

The only cure that Alcoholics Anonymous provides is, 'literally', a miracle. *(all references are from Step Six).*

Step Seven: Humbly asked Him to remove our shortcomings.

Alcoholics Anonymous declares that religion has nothing to do with its Steps, but in reality it is the foundation of all of the Twelve Steps and cannot be separated out; *"The attainment of greater humility is the foundation principle of each of AA's Twelve Steps... That basic ingredient of all humility"* is *"a desire to seek and do God's will"* *(Step 7)*.

AA bills itself as a program of suggestions rather than requirements; *"All of its Twelve Steps are but suggestions (Step 2).* AA, though, puts lie to that by instituting the 'necessity' of seeking and doing God's will; *"So it is we first see humility as a necessity" (Step 7).*

AA claims secularism. On the contrary, AA here directs the member to ask the Christian God to perform a miracle. AA has admitted in Step Six that God is meant literally (see above), and they have defined their 'character defects' as the Seven

Deadly Sins of ancient Christian theology (see Step Four above). Now AA directs us to, with a *"a desire to seek and do God's will"*, ask God to remove these Seven Deadly Sins.

This Step serves as the climax, of the search for our Seven Deadly Sins, by mandating participation in the AAs ritual equivalent to being Born Again

Steps Eight & Nine; Made a list of all persons we had harmed, and became willing to make amends to them all; Made direct amends to such people wherever possible, except when to do so would injure them or others.

There are really no particularly religious exercises in these two Steps, except for the fact that they are part of the overall program. Drinking juice in church isn't in itself a religious activity- but your still at church.

Step Ten: Continued to take personal inventory and when we were wrong promptly admitted it.

Alcoholics Anonymous swears that their program is not religious. In this Step, though, AA increases the amount of prayer to their living, healing God. The program dictates that each member will pray several times daily (and more), searching themselves for the Seven Deadly Sins; *"a continuous look at our assets and liabilities...are necessities...no one can make much of his life until self-searching becomes a regular habit... There's the spot-check inventory, taken at any time of the day, whenever we find ourselves getting tangled up. There's one we take at day's end...Many AAs go in for annual or semi-annual housecleanings. Many also like the experience of an occasional retreat"* (Step 10).

This Step directs deeper involvement in the supernatural. Having previously defined their 'inventory' as a member's search for how they have committed the Seven Deadly Sins (see Step Four, above), they now direct their members to perform that ritual multiple times daily.

Step Eleven: Sought through prayer and meditation to improve our conscious contact with God as we understood Him, praying only for knowledge of His will for us and the power to carry that out.

AA claims that it is "god as we understand Him", but this Step prepares us for Step Twelve, where AA admits that it has been lying, and that AA was designed to correct our misconceptions; *"The persistent use of meditation and prayer, we found, did open a channel"* to *"God as we were increasingly better able to understand Him... the doubter... who still considered his well-loved AA group the higher power, would presently love God and call Him by name" (Step 12).*

AA has called itself a program of suggestions, but in this Step they declare their faith-healing dogma "facts"; *"We all need the light of God's reality, the nourishment of His strength, and the atmosphere of His grace. To an amazing extent the facts of AA life confirm this ageless truth" (Step 11).* The "facts" of AA life, not the 'suggestions'.

Alcoholics Anonymous posits this Step as not religious but makes clear this Step's intensely religious goal; speaking of meditation, AA asserts that *"...its object is always the same: to improve our conscious contact with God, with His grace, wisdom and love" (Step 11).*

Again, Alcoholics Anonymous claims secularism while announcing this Step's intensely religious nature. AA also eliminates any possible secular interpretation of the word 'meditation'; *"Now, what of prayer? Prayer is the raising of the heart and mind to God- and in this sense it includes meditation (Step 11).*

In Step 11, Alcoholics Anonymous effectively announces that it has been lying about the religious nature of AA.

Step Twelve: Having had a spiritual awakening as a result of these steps, we tried to carry this message to alcoholics, and to practice these principles in all our affairs.

Alcoholics Anonymous insists publicly that there is nothing religious about their program. On the contrary, in Step Twelve, AA has defined their 'spiritual awakening' as intensely religious and instructs their members to hide this religion from their recruiting targets.

AA defines their 'spiritual awakening' in both 12x12 book and the Big Book; "*The persistent use of meditation and prayer, we found, did open the channel so that where there had been a trickle, there now was a river which led to sure power and safe guidance from God as we were increasingly better able to understand Him. So, practicing these Steps, we had a spiritual awakening about which finally there was no question... we could predict that the doubter... who still considered his well-loved AA group the higher power, would presently love God and call Him by name*" (12x12, Step 12). Even more explicitly, AA describes the deeply religious nature of the awakening in Big Book chapter 'We Agnostics''; "*One night, he was approached by an alcoholic who had known a spiritual experience. Our friends gorge rose as he bitterly cried out: 'If there is a God, He certainly hasn't done anything for me'.... Then, like a thunderbolt, a great thought came. It crowded out all else. 'Who are you to say there is no God?' This man recounts that he tumbled out of bed to his knees. In a few seconds he was overwhelmed by a*

113

conviction of the Presence of God. It poured over and through him... He stood in the Presence of Infinite Power and Love. He had stepped from bridge to shore. For the first time, he lived in conscious companionship with his Creator". This is what Alcoholics Anonymous sells to the world as "not religious", and they give explicit instructions to their members to swear that their program is secular while they fulfill the other half of Step Twelve; proselytizing.

Alcoholics Anonymous likes to hold forth on how honest they are, but they explicitly direct their members to conceal the program's religion. In the 12x12 chapter on Step Two, AA labels non-believers as 'belligerent savages' and, in the Big Book chapter 'Working With Others', denounces those non-believers' beliefs as "prejudiced" and "confused". AA instructs their recruiters to "use everyday language to describe spiritual principles. There is no use arousing any prejudice he may have against certain theological terms and conceptions about which he may already be confused. Don't raise such issues... Let him see that you are not there to instruct him in religion" (Big Book, 'Working With Others)

CHAPTER 5
The Danger of A.A.

Well, I have laid out the indoctrination of Alcoholics Anonymous to the best of my ability and I hope everyone will find it of interest.

While I was writing this book, my mind sometimes wandered, as all of ours do sometimes. I sometimes considered the plight of Charlie Sheen.

I don't know, and have never met or spoken to, Charlie Sheen and am no more privy to his experience than anyone else; I only know what I've seen on TV, on-line or in printed media. However, my experience with getting ground-up in the substance abuse treatment mill gives me a certain perspective and a certain amount of sympathy for Mr. Sheen. Arguably the most successful actor in modern times (everything the man touches turns into gold), when he started having problems with substance abuse he found himself thrown down the same rabbit hole as so many before him. His case was special, though; because he was such a public figure, and the star of number one television show, the pressure on him to conform to substance abuse treatment protocols was immense. I believe it was this pressure that led to his freaking out on those close to him. His close friends and associates didn't realize that, when they pushed him towards treatment, they had pushed him to be a faith-healing fundamentalist Christian. If they had known what the true goal of treatment was- indoctrination- they would have left him alone.

What was publicly derided as Mr. Sheen's meltdown was actually, I believe, his reaction to everyone in his life (and in his case, that also includes the public) telling him that he had to turn into a faith-healing, fundamentalist Christian who would agree to thump the bible of Alcoholics Anonymous. Because AA's successful public relations campaign has fooled people into believing that their religion is legitimate medicine, as opposed to the fundamentalist religion that it is, Mr. Sheen had no chance of defending himself. His only choice was to conform to AA or be condemned. I believe his widely publicized outbursts during that period were his reactions to this dilemma. Remember, he was being subjected to all of this in the public spotlight; when I went through this I was just a guy but with Mr. Sheen it's different.

When I was told that I was living my life wrong, it was kind of hard to argue with. But Mr. Sheen?- we're talking about the Man. I would ask the reader to put themselves in his shoes; you've succeeded at life like so few people have. You're famous, well- liked, filthy rich, and you sleep with (and sometimes marry) some of the most beautiful women in the world. You're such a good guy that even when you shoot one of your wives in the arm, she has only good things to say about you. For your entire adult life you've had enough money to buy anything you want- food, booze, houses, women, drugs and just about anything else you fancy. Then, you got older. It catches everyone by surprise, but it does catch everyone; you just can't do all of the things you used to be able to do.

When I was a youngun' I could work all day, drink and get high all night, then go to work again the next day without a problem. Now that I'm older, I can't even stay up late anymore. We could see the same thing happen to Mr. Sheen. All of the sudden, his partying was giving him problems at work- he's an old man, after all. When public and professional pressure started building on him to get help, he probably did seek help.... and ran into the brick wall of Alcoholics Anonymous. Can anyone who has read this book see any way that disaster wouldn't result?

Here's a man who is one of the most successful people in history, both personally and professionally, who has developed one problem; drinking and getting high have gotten out of hand. Now, in order to address that single issue, he's told that he has to turn into a faith-healing Christian who proselytizes for Alcoholics Anonymous and who can never have another drop of alcohol for the rest of his life. If he tried to protest such ridiculous suggestions and demands, he would have been told that that just means he's really sick, that it's just his disease talking, that he just needs to pray harder. There's no way to exit that death spiral; the more you object to forced religious indoctrination, the deeper they try to shove that indoctrination down your throat. There exists only one other choice, and I believe that me and Mr. Sheen both took that choice, albeit in different ways; we told them to git bit. I did it by suing, Mr. Sheen did it with his Torpedo Of Truth tour (I think my course was more successful). In any event, I believe the forced indoctrination program of Alcoholics Anonymous, however directly or indirectly, cost Mr. Sheen his 'Two and a Half Men' role.

Therein lies the problem. We as a people have allowed Alcoholics Anonymous to take control of our lives. Sure, we're free to pray as we choose, or to not pray at all, but only until someone in power decides that they've had enough of that nonsense.

We live in a world where every person with any authority has the right to take samples of our bodies- urine, hair, spit, DNA. Anyone with authority over us now has the right to dictate what we are allowed to put in our bodies and how we manage our bodies. Employers may test for both legal and illegal drugs and, if they decide to institute a relevant policy, may require us to live according to their rules.

I can remember when I was a child and the discussions were just starting about workplace drug screening. People who in favor of allowing that intrusion always fell back on the tired old saw "If you're not doing anything wrong, you don't have anything to worry about". What I find to be quite ironic about that is that many of the people who spouted that defense were cigarette smokers; that attitude is now coming back to bite smokers, and others, right in the butt.

I remember those who so objected to that new development as doing so more on macro-philosophical grounds rather than any specific threat to our freedoms; the objection mainly rested on the philosophy that we should not have to surrender our bodies in order to maintain employment. Their concerns were pooh-poohed away; after all, the invasion of privacy was small, what's the big deal? Alcoholics Anonymous has proven what the big deal is.

In Cleveland Ohio, the Cleveland Clinic is one of the largest, if not the largest, employers in Cleveland. They have now extended drug screening to include tobacco, a perfectly legal, non-impairing drug. Nicotine will have absolutely no effect on those employees' ability to perform their job but the Cleveland Clinic will screen out all smokers in the pre-employment drug screen. Currently, there is no effect on those already employed, but that stands only at the whim of the Cleveland Clinic. Now, consider the implications of this.

Alcoholics Anonymous has spread out far beyond alcohol. Today, you can find just-about-anything Anonymous for whatever the bad habit of the day is. Because employers have so much say over our bodies, and because Alcoholics Anonymous so successfully pretends to be non-religious medical treatment, just about anyone can be ordered into their churches. The potential for abuse is vast; in this instance, Cleveland Clinic employees could be forced into the Twelve Step 'Nicotine Anonymous', whose program rings a bell;

The Twelve Steps of Nicotine Anonymous

1. We admitted we were powerless over nicotine – that our lives had become unmanageable.

2. Came to believe that a Power greater than ourselves could restore us to sanity.

3. Made a decision to turn our will and our lives over to the care of God as we understood Him.

4. Made a searching and fearless moral inventory of ourselves.

5. Admitted to God, to ourselves, and to another human being the exact nature of our wrongs.

6. Were entirely ready to have God remove all these defects of character.

7. Humbly asked Him to remove our shortcomings.

8. Made a list of all persons we had harmed, and became willing to make amends to them all.

9. Made direct amends to such people wherever possible, except when to do so would injure them or others.

10. Continued to take personal inventory and when we were wrong promptly admitted it.

11. Sought through prayer and meditation to improve our conscious contact with God as we understood Him, praying only for knowledge of His will for us and the power to carry that out.

12. Having had a spiritual awakening as the result of these steps, we tried to carry this message to nicotine users and to practice these principles in all our affairs

As long as AA is able to keep passing itself off as secular, companies like the Cleveland Clinic can order their employees into AA pews with impunity. When they expand their no-nicotine policy to their current employees, those employees can be forced into the same merry-go-round that alcoholics are forced into; the Clinic could require attendance at Nicotine Anonymous meetings and professional treatment personnel could require attendance at NA meetings on threat of failing them, hence getting them fired and rendering them incapable of supporting their families. There is no recourse; because these Twelve Step programs enjoy immunity from the U.S. Constitution, anyone can be forced into them- anyone. And it doesn't stop with smokers.

Dr. Toby Cosgrove, Cleveland Clinic Chief Executive, also said that he would not hire overweight people if he could legally avoid it. There are companies so concerned about the extra cost of healthcare for the overweight that they are threatening economic sanctions against people with some extra meat on their bones. And, wouldn't you know it, there's also an Overeaters Anonymous. And their program seems oddly familiar;

The Twelve Steps of Overeaters Anonymous

1. We admitted we were powerless over food — that our lives had become unmanageable.
2. Came to believe that a Power greater than ourselves could restore us to sanity.
3. Made a decision to turn our will and our lives over to the care of God as we understood Him.
4. Made a searching and fearless moral inventory of ourselves.
5. Admitted to God, to ourselves and to another human being the exact nature of our wrongs.
6. Were entirely ready to have God remove all these defects of character.
7. Humbly asked Him to remove our shortcomings.
8. Made a list of all persons we had harmed and became willing to make amends to them all.

9. Made direct amends to such people wherever possible, except when to do so would injure them or others.

10. Continued to take personal inventory and when we were wrong, promptly admitted it.

11. Sought through prayer and meditation to improve our conscious contact with God as we understood Him, praying only for knowledge of His will for us and the power to carry that out.

12. Having had a spiritual awakening as the result of these Steps, we tried to carry this message to compulsive overeaters and to practice these principles in all our affairs

I think it's clear to see that every bad habit or excessive indulgence can have the Twelve Steps of Alcoholics Anonymous grafted on to it. If Alcoholics Anonymous is allowed to continue passing their faith-healing off as medicine, no American's freedom of conscience is safe. We are all a drink, pound or a puff away from getting ordered to church.

CHAPTER 6
My Story of Self-Cure

I have heard consistently is that alcoholism is an incurable disease that only Alcoholics Anonymous can provide an answer to; I am living proof that that is untrue. I rejected the entire disease model (with extreme prejudice, I might add) while in my twenties and have not had an alcohol related problem since; I am now in my fifties. I believe what I did can work for almost anyone.

I was born in Chicago to a father who ran away, a paranoid schizophrenic mother and two brothers, one of which thought trying to kill me with a pillow was great sport (though he never really bothered me after I threw the dining room table at his head. It wasn't a bad shot either- he got lucky). I grew up in slums and never really had a future to look forward to.

I started drinking and getting high at around twelve or thirteen years of age and by the time I was a grown man, I had tried- and quite enjoyed- most drugs that were available back then. In my mid-twenties, things started taking a turn for the worse. Not horrible, but enough to end up on probation for DWI.

It was at about that time that I started to run into alcohol related problems. If you look at the federal lawsuits that I was involved in, to halt forced AA, you'll find 3 driving offenses. That's a little misleading; at that time, in the State of New York, Driving While Impaired was not a crime, but rather just a violation. My first two arrests were only at that level while my third and final offense was a crime, Driving While Intoxicated (the police officer even told me "You know just how much to drink"- my three Blood Alcohol Content level were .09, .09 and .1, a nice grouping). That DWI earned for me my soon to be problematic order to attend AA, along with alcohol treatment, during my three years of probation.

Earlier in the book, I explained my federal lawsuit so I won't bother detailing that again; that's not where I've been heading with this anyway. The important part of this is to explain that with my rejection of AA, and a rejection of the idea that I am 'addicted', I've not had an alcohol related problem in decades. As I type this, I've been working on this book for about one month and I've drank exactly one can of beer- not because I'm sitting here denying myself but because that's all that I've wanted. If you want to call that a 'cure', go ahead. I look at it from a different angle but I know one thing for sure; I'm in a place better than any AAer could ever dream of- I don't drink to satisfy a need.

That's my point. I now drink like any normal human being. The whole idea that the way to handle drug and alcohol problems is by demanding immediate and complete life- long abstinence just doesn't make sense.

When most people get to the point of being a persistent drug or alcohol problem to the law, the offender has probably been imbibing for years, if not decades. Every approach towards 'recovery' that I've ever heard fails to take that into account. I don't care what approach you take; if you tell a man that has been drinking for twenty years that, right now, he must stop drinking and never touch another drop- NEVER- you are *almost* certainly doomed to failure because *habits* don't disappear that easy. There is also the man's logic to take into account.

One of the problems with the AA approach is that it's overkill. When a person gets a DWI, the DWI is the problem that needs to be addressed. We can talk until we're blue in the face, but we will never get past that logic. The man in question will always figure that he can get away with driving after he's had a few; when he gets arrested again, he'll still keep that logic. THAT'S what needs to be addressed; once you can get through to this man that there will *always* be the risk of getting caught (what if someone hit's him? What if he comes across a roadblock? Etc...) and that the consequences just aren't worth it, society's chances of this man obeying its laws will improve sharply.

If we take the concepts of God and addiction

out of the discussion, we can approach the problem on a purely human basis. When a person has been drinking long term, that is a pattern of behavior that must be broken. AA approaches the problem by demanding an instant, life-long commitment to never drink- forever- by promising a miracle from the Creator. Is that a reasonable request? I think not. What is needed is an approach which has a reasonable chance of success.

The habit of drinking can only broken by not drinking. If you demand life-long sobriety, you're asking more than you have a right to. But if you explain that you need the patient to stop drinking- absolute sobriety- for a <u>finite</u> period of around six months, then that is something that you have a good chance at achieving.

Honesty is of the utmost importance here. If you try to get the patient to believe that that six-month sober period is all that he has to do and then change that later, he'll know you tricked him, like Alcoholics Anonymous. You must be honest and make him a full partner, and for good reason; this is not the seeking of a miracle, it is the changing of patterns. The patient has to know exactly what is going on, because it is *his* mental work that effects that change.

This finite approach also targets a specific problem with Alcoholics Anonymous treatment; AA is a one size fits all approach. If a person has but *one* alcohol related incident, they are told that they can never again have even one drink and must convert to faith-healing Christianity. What I suggest is actually targeting the problem itself.

What I'm proposing is simple; have the patient go for as long as he can without drinking, than he can go ahead and drink, but he should drink as little as he can be content. Then, just keep repeating that cycle. Make him a complete and knowing partner in this endeavor; make sure he knows that the idea is for each cycle to see lower alcohol consumption. The point is not to increase his ability to resist, but rather decrease his desire to the point that there is no *urge*. This is what I did, though I didn't have a concrete plan at the time. I eventually lost the "urge" to drink, though I occasionally imbibe. I haven't been intoxicated in years. But this cannot be a con job; the patient has to understand the method and the goal.

I have no illusions that this is necessarily as easy for others as it was for me, and for some the first cycle or two may need to be supervised, but it *must* be in full partnership and with the full participation of the patient. He *must* know what he's doing and he *must* be trying to change his own mindset. Otherwise, he's just taking a break before he goes back to drinking full tilt. I believe that this will work for almost any human behavior that a person wants to change, except those that are true addictions such as heroin.

Humans can change their own habits and patterns. Except in rare cases I don't believe that 'alcoholism' is an addiction; it is a habit reinforced within the patient's mind over the course of years by the pleasure that alcohol provides. We don't need God; we need structured breaks from alcohol that we can consciously expand until we no longer have urges for alcohol, but we aren't afraid to have a beer. We also will not be addicted to faith-healing rituals.

The End

23707425R00073

Made in the USA
Lexington, KY
20 June 2013